Pecans-Volume II

A Grower's Perspective

G. Wesley Rice
Ponca City, OK 74604

On the Cover

Top – A commercial pecan orchard near Columbia, Missouri – owned and operated by George Montgomery. This well managed operation illustrates that pecans can be successfully grown in Agricultural Zone 5 with proper cultivar selection and management practices. The author and Mr. Montgomery are "holding down" the tractor.

Left – Mechanical harvest helps to get crops into protected space quickly. Mechanical cleaning equipment can be used to separate debris and poorly filled nuts from the edible portion of the harvest. See pages 133 to 135 for further information.

Bottom – Many pecan orchards and groves are family operations. The younger Rice family grandsons (Josh, Robbie and Ethan) spend happy times in the orchard gathering pecans, looking at wildlife, and enjoying nature. Ethan, the youngest, says that pecan dirt is mighty tasty! The two older grandsons, Craig and Brandon, were featured on the cover of my earlier book. The younger ones have demanded equal attention. See the chapter "Pecaning" for further information.

The photo-op of the Rice Grandsons on the tractor is a reminder that children should be closely supervised when around farm equipment. Likewise, adults should remember that safety issues should receive top priority when operating farm equipment.

ISBN: 09656644-3-0 – Hard Cover

ISBN: 09656644-4-9 – Perfect Bound

To all the pecan enthusiasts who made my first pecan book a success.

iv

Contents

Cultivar List

Acknowledgments

This book, although written from a grower's perspective, has developed from th´teachings of pecan specialists and others across the country. I applaud those listed below, and others too numerous to mention, for their expert guidance, patience, and advice. In addition to these specialist, I also voice my appreciation to growers and others for contributions in both know-how and sometimes sympathy when natural and man-made disasters struck my orchard.

Pecan Specialists

- Dr. Phillip Mulder, Oklahoma State University
- Dr. Michael Smith, Oklahoma State University
- Dr. Sharon von Brombsen, Oklahoma State University
- Dr. Glen "Cat" Taylor, Oklahoma State University, Noble Foundation, Retired
- Dr. Dean McCraw, Oklahoma State University, Retired
- Dr. Raymond Eikenbary, Oklahoma State University, Retired
- Ms. Becky Carroll, Oklahoma State University
- Dr. Kenneth Hunt, University of Missouri
- Dr. William Reid, Kansas State University
- Dr. Bill Goff, Auburn University
- Ms. Cathy Browne, Auburn University
- Mr. Troy Pabst, University of Nebraska at Lincoln
- Dr. Tommy Thompson, USDA-ARS, College Station, Texas
- Dr. Bill Ree, Texas Agricultural Extension Service

Historian

- Ms. Gladys Kitchen, Pawnee, Oklahoma

Growers

- Mr. Joe Reinert, Blackwell, Oklahoma
- Mr. Dick Hoffman, Stillwater, Oklahoma
- Mr. Gary Fernald, Monmouth, Illinois
- Mr. George Montgomery, Columbia, Missouri

Photographic Credits

Highlights from
Pecans - A Grower's Perspective
(Volume I, New Edition)

To address the desires of those who have requested copies of my first pecan book, now out of print, I have elected to include key elements of my first book in this manuscript. These pages will provide continuity for those who have read my previous works, and hopefully will provide some useful information for my first-time readers. I have included color plates for most of the cultivar selections in the first book, except for a few that I've deemed unworthy of consideration. I'm sure, however, that many of my readers will have differing opinions. Improved versions of other pictures, including insect pests, disease illustrations, and other relevant items are also included. I have elected to include these pictures <u>as a part of Volume II</u>, allowing for what I feel is a more easily understood organization of the material.

Chapters Included in Volume I – New Edition

1. Pecaning

2. Book Overview and Organization

3. Pecans – Facts and Fairy Tales

4. Pecan – The Tree

5. Getting Started

6. On-Going Management

7. Pecan Varieties

8. Propagation

9. Pest and Disease Management

10. Nutrition and Watering Requirements

11. Pecans for Food

Synopsis of Volume I

The topics listed on the previous page describe the general contents of my first pecan book, _Pecans- A Grower's Perspective._ Although the book has been out of print for some time, it is available from many libraries across the country. The following highlights, organized by chapter, will provide the reader with items to consider when growing pecans. More detail on the various topics can be found in the reference material also listed in this section. Your County Extension Agricultural Agent is typically an excellent resource in learning about pecan culture. Your agent has access to many of the university based pecan specialists and others across the country.

Besides the technical aspects of pecan growing, I take pride in exploring the human element associated with pecan culture. Many of the orchards and groves across the country are managed and operated by individual families. It's rewarding to see family members working together to make their pecan business a success. I've provided pecan products and services for over 20 years. I've never hesitated to send out products and provide services prior to receiving compensation for them. I've never lost a penny! I've found pecan people to be hard working, honest, and dependable. I've also dealt with pecan specialists in the USDA, in our universities, and other places. I've found them to be helpful and considerate of my needs — whether they're in Oklahoma or elsewhere.

Some of us who are "nuts about pecans", may have been inflicted with a pecaning disorder. We are often out in the orchard at night, when we ought to be asleep. Some of us have missed the Super Bowl on TV only to find ourselves in the orchard fighting both the snow and a chain saw. At least we can be glad that pecaning isn't often fatal.

For those of you who have read and studied my first pecan volume, most of what I scripted still holds true today — some ten years after the date of the first publication. New cultivars, pesticides, and other technologies have augmented material in my first book. Government and other regulations have removed some pesticides that were appropriate for pecans. The ever evolving disease strains have altered the natural resistance of some cultivars. Thus. pecan culture is a dynamic process. Still, the orchard is perhaps the best living laboratory for evaluating both old technology and the new processes that have been introduced in these past ten years, and for the years beyond.

Cultivar Names in Single Quotes

Recent nomenclature suggests that cultivar names be enclosed in single quotes: 'Pawnee', for example. Since this form of designation was not in place when my first book was published, I have elected not to use the single quote designation in the Volume I Highlights section. I have, however, used the single quote convention in new portions of the book.

Chapter 1

PECANING

Webster defines *pecan* as "a form of hickory tree or nut thereof, indigenous to the lower Mississippi valley and grown in the southern U. S. for its oval smooth shelled nut having a sweet, oily, edible kernel." It follows then that PECANING is the act of acquiring pecans. This act can be accomplished by growing your own, picking pecans on the shares, purchasing them, etc. It can be one of the memorable family activities that enhances the bond between father, son, grandson, and other family members.

Some of my fondest memories are trips which involved "pecaning" with my grandsons. The episode described below was more than a decade ago. For some reason at age seventeen, Brandon thinks that girls and his electric guitar are more interesting than pecans. A particular trip, described in my first book, is especially memorable. Brandon was five then, and the following description says it all:

The morning broke clear and crisp. Vestiges of orange and yellow highlighted remnants of clouds in the east as if put there by some magic paint brush. The south wind and humidity had given way to northerly breezes that had subsided over the night to at least a tolerable 10-15 Miles per hour. The new fallen leaves crunched under our feet as we made our way to that special tree scouted earlier in the summer. A few other early birds (people and other forms of pecan consumers) were also arriving, but so far only a squirrel was near our tree to compete for the bounty. Brandon hurried along, and broke into a run. "I see a bunch," he said, and hurried to start filling his sack. Last year, experience and grandfatherly guidance taught the art and science of differentiating good pecans from bad pecans. Brandon was now as adept as a fox squirrel at rejecting weevil infested and other poor quality nuts. The day ended with half full sacks. The mid-morning autumn sun had forced us to shed the first of three layers of clothing. It peeked through remnants of yellow and gold leaves painted magically by earlier frosts. Many of their once green predecessors had yielded to the brisk winds of the past evening, and to the elements of wind and rain of the past weeks. A raspy call marked the presence of a retreating blue jay. It held a pecan securely in it's beak, showing that man was not the only creature adept at pecaning.

Besides grandsons, there's the family dog. I would like to say that even dogs can inherit the pecaning disorder, but some people might think that I must have eaten too many pecans — or had too much of something else. Katie, our half beagle/half border collie also loves pecans, pecan trees, and of course the squirrels that go with them. She can crack even the toughest native pecans with her teeth, eat the kernels, and spit out the shells. This miraculous act can take place either under the pecan tree or on the living room carpet. I guess some things such as pecans and watermelon taste better to a dog if eaten on something soft.

A Living laboratory. The orchard is a living laboratory that documents the many actions and interactions of a microenvironment that centers around the pecan/hickory ecology. Critters such as the pecan weevil live only in this environment. Squirrels and other pecan predators can sense better than humans when pecans are barely ripe enough to be edible. They cart off good pecans and let the bad ones lie.

Proper management of a pecan orchard requires an in-depth knowledge of this microenvironment and the living and inanimate objects that go along with it. Knowledge that is initiated through reading and listening is reinforced and "learned" through practice and observation in the orchard. The orchard is where many new concepts are tried not solely for the sake of science, but at the financial risk of the grower whose next meal is contingent on his orchard's success rather than failure. Like pioneers who gave up the security of the known to try something that had the potential to be better, pecan people are always willing to test new cultivars and new methods. The orchard is where the facts are truly separated from the fairy tales.

Chapter 2
BOOK OVERVIEW

This book covers both human interest episodes and technical information. In some ways, the human interest parts illustrate the practical side of learning the technology. After all, experience has proven to be an adept teacher. What we learn from experience is usually not soon forgotten. Many of the findings and statements in this book are thus based on actual experience and observations. Like all pecan growers and researchers, my likes and dislikes differ to some extent from those of others. Perhaps the most important thing that I've learned is that pecans are often mysterious and unpredictable - or so they seem to be. Dr. Glen "Cat" Taylor, a well known pecan specialist in Oklahoma, said as he reviewed Volume I: "— About the time we think we understand the pecan, and how to manipulate it to our advantage, the rules start to change. Pecans can dent your pride, cause humbling moments, and challenge credibility." The same pecan cultivar will behave differently in the various geographical locations. Thus there are almost no absolutes, only degrees of variation.

A Grower's Perspective

What is the relevance of writing with a grower's perspective? I thought about this question a lot. Information is information whether it comes from the grower or from specialists in the various fields that relate to pecans. Perhaps one difference is that the grower has a slightly different risk threshold. When a grower experiments with something new, failures are reflected in the bank balance. For the researcher, failures are an expected part of learning.

After considerable thought, I feel that the statement **"good enough"** is the most relevant difference between recommendations from the grower and recommendations from the various pecan specialists.

Good Enough. Growing pecans to perfection requires at least a 36 hour day, and 500 days per year. There are always more things to be done than there is time to perform the tasks. When reading technical literature, I find myself skimming over parts of the information. I think, "that sounds like a good idea – if I could afford the time or afford the cost." Another reason for skimming over the literature is that it doesn't register the first time around. I get bogged down in technical details. I skip over the whole thing with unfounded hopes of reading it again later. This can be dangerous if three or four critical processes are buried somewhere in the technical detail.

I've attended lots of seminars on time management and other technical issues in my former career. Many of the revelations that seemed important when I attended these seminars have long since been forgotten. One concept has stuck with me over the years. The concept is **"good enough."** Many specialists provide the way to do things perfectly. After all, that's their job. There is certainly nothing wrong with perfection. The problem is finding the time to do all things perfectly. Sometimes, good enough is all that we have time to accomplish. Better to do things good enough than not to do them at all. The "not at all" syndrome is all too common in growing pecans.

Qualifications and Opinions. I'm sure many of you are wondering, "When there are so many pecan specialists around, why should a grower from Oklahoma write a book on pecans?" I'll be the first to admit that most of the specialists that I've consulted have forgotten more about the respective facets of pecan husbandry than I will ever know. Perhaps the main thing that I have to offer is that I am a grower like many of the readers of this book. I have read, studied, and consulted with many of the leading experts on pecans. Relevant data and techniques have been assimilated and tried in a real world environment.

One of the main things that I've learned to do is to prioritize. I can't spend 90% of my time accomplishing 10% of the benefit of improving pecan health and habitat. This philosophy gets back to "good enough." Back in my other career as a geophysicist, I always griped at my employees for trying to fine tune trivial decisions, while not trying hard enough to solve problems that really mattered. I should have griped at myself also. I know that in my own orchard, too much time is spent on things that I like to do, and too little time is spent on yucky chores like spraying. I hate spraying with a purple passion. Seems like I tell myself that it is too wet, too windy, too early or too late to spray. Even worse, I listen to myself! Thus, my spray program is about half of what it should be. If I followed all the guidelines in my book, my pecan production and quality would be better. So I also know what many growers like and what they dislike. I have stated many things in this book that are based on observation and opinion. If I see it happen, I'm more inclined to believe it. Most of my statements and recommendations are also tempered with a second opinion from someone who is entitled to give one. I feel that this approach is better than quoting third hand indirect observations. Too often, comments are made and information is conveyed without the benefit of personal observation and verification.

I know of instances where comments on specific cultivars were passed from one person to another. The same statement thus made it into several separate references written by different people. Come to find out, the cultivar was mis-identified. The information was correct, only it was about the wrong cultivar. Think about what would happen if somebody mis-identified a dog as a cat. We would see a reference like: "Dogs make wonderful pets. They use a litterbox and are easily trained. It's tough though to keep them from climbing to the top of the highest tree." In a similar fashion, the cultivar ID problem conveyed that a very scab prone cultivar was resistant to scab, among other things.

Problems arise also from assuming that pecans of the same variety behave the same irregardless of location and climate. One year, Colby may mature ahead of Peruque. The next year in the same orchard, Peruque may mature before Colby. Cultivar properties are especially subject to geographical and climactic variations. Wichita behaves differently in southern Texas than it does in northern Oklahoma. Lucas behaves differently in southern Ontario than in Nebraska. And so on.

Thus the moral of the story is to look at general ranges of behavior rather than exact and precise events that happen from year to year. Averages over a period of several years will often be more useful than a single observation. Also, judgments about cultivar performance should be based on several separate trees. Location in the orchard, rootstock, and other variables can significantly affect performance. I once made a bad assumption that Shawnee lacked cold tolerance because a single tree had problems. Later, Shawnee propagated onto other native rootstock showed good freeze resistance.

Geographical Considerations

Much of the information in this book is independent of geographical location. Pecan tree anatomy changes little from place to place. Leaves, tree structure, flowers, and other parts of the tree look generally the same in all areas. Pecan cultivars look generally the same irregardless of where they're grown. Pecan pests look much the same whether they're in Missouri or in Florida.

Growth habits and tree characteristics for a given cultivar do, however, vary to some extent depending on where they're planted. Also, different cultivars are more suited to some locations than others. An improper cultivar selection significantly reduces the chances of success in growing pecans. The map and descriptions on pages 48-51 show preferred cultivars for different geographical zones. In the future, this list is sure to change. New cultivars will be added; some current recommended cultivars will be dropped.

The arrow on the map indicates the location of my pecan operation. I am fortunate that my location is at the juncture of three pecan zones, allowing me to test a wide variety of cultivars in a single environment. Nut maturity dates, flowering dates, and other data were collected from this location.

Some significant variations in ecological conditions and pecan culture exist in these major pecan zones. It's good to identify the zone where you will be growing pecans, and note any special requirements for the area. Soil conditions, average rainfall, humidity levels, temperature extremes, and other factors vary significantly across pecan country. Although cultural practices and recommendations for these different areas are mentioned throughout the book, some highlights for major geographical zones are introduced below:

Northern Pecan Zones

1. This area relates to the north and far north areas of the map on page 51. See the list of recommended cultivars for these areas.

2. Use cold hardy northern rootstock.

3. Soils generally vary in pH from slightly acidic to slightly alkaline. See **Chapter 10** for nutritional recommendations, including zinc application.

4. Rainfall and subsurface water are generally sufficient to grow pecans without irrigation. Supplemental water during dry periods is needed for best performance.

5. The major pecan pests are native to many parts of the area, and must be managed to produce quality pecans and healthy trees.

6. A fungicide program may be necessary in the more humid regions for disease susceptible cultivars.

Central Zones

1. This area relates to the central and east central zones on the page 51 map. Avoid using late maturing cultivars. Anything that matures later than Stuart will not reliably ripen before the first fall freeze.

2. Cold hardy root stock is recommended.

3. Temperature extremes are conducive to cold injury.

4. Soil pH is variable. Determine soil pH for your location. Note proper nutritional procedures in **Chapter 10**.

5. Soil moisture and rainfall are typically adequate to maintain pecan tree life. Apply supplemental water during dry periods for best performance.

6. All significant pecan pests inhabit this area and must be managed to achieve tree health and nut quality.

Southern Pecan Zones

1. See pages 48 on, for recommended cultivars for the southeastern and south-central zones. Avoid cultivars that are highly susceptible to scab.

2. A comprehensive disease control program is essential in the southeastern zone, and may be required for some cultivars in the south-central zone.

3. Major pests are present in the southeastern and south-central zones. An integrated pest management program is an essential management procedure.

4. Rainfall generally increases from west to east. Although soil moisture and rainfall will sustain pecan growth over most of the area, irrigation during dry periods will improve crop yield and quality.

5. Soils vary in pH; however, the southeastern zone typically has acidic soil. See the chapter **"Nutrition and Water Requirements"** for further information.

6. These zones usually have little trouble with nut maturity for all listed cultivars. Freeze injury and sticktights are, however, potential problems to be dealt with from time to time.

Western Pecan Zones

1. Western and Wichita are the primary cultivars for this region. See pages 61-71 for other adapted cultivars. Damages from scab and other pecan diseases are minimal.

Disclaimers and Such

In today's society of lawyers and law suits, I will go on record as not being responsible for your orchard, grove, and yard planting failures. Also, if all your pecan weevils die from spray, I just hope for both our sakes that their great and powerful pecan weevil lawyer (a pecan weevil trained in law) goes down with them. At least I would want a jury of growers in preference to one comprised of angry pecan weevils. If a crow gets choked on a pecan that it steals from your orchard, hopefully you won't be sued by an environmentalist somewhere. If a squirrel gets a tummy ache from eating 10 pounds of your green

Peruque nuts, hopefully you won't have to pay its doctor bill.

Similarly, I won't take credit for your successes either. I won't demand ten percent of your pecan crop, just because you followed my advice — and I have done my best to provide sound advice. Key chapters have been previewed by experts in the various subjects. The book is as good as I know how to make it. But pecan culture is subject to changes. Growers need to adapt to new and better technology as it evolves. New and better techniques will likely replace some of the standards of today, and they in turn will be replaced at a later date. This is progress and we pecan growers need to take advantage of all the progress that comes along. I hope that my book is both entertaining and informative. May your pecan nuts be large, solid, and tasty, and your pecan trees green, healthy, and central leader oriented. Happy reading!!

Chapter 3
PECANS — FACTS AND FAIRY TALES

Originating in North America, pecans have a prominent place in history. They provided sustenance to Native Americans and many early European explorers. Both as a commercial food source and a tree that beautifies yards and gardens across America and other places around the world, pecans are many things to many people. In my years of studying pecans and pecan culture, I have heard and read many tales, stories, and facts. Some have proven to be truths; others have proven to exist only in the minds of the story tellers. When growing pecans both for fun and for profit, it is important to separate the facts from the fairy tales.

Pecan Origins

Pecans are a product of North America. The native range extends from Mexico to as far north as Illinois and Iowa. Native pecans are found in Texas, Oklahoma, Louisiana, Mississippi, Arkansas, Missouri, Kansas, Tennessee, Kentucky, Illinois, and Iowa. For thousands of years, pecans were known only to Native Americans. Spanish explorers in the early 1500's noted the existence of pecans. They described pecans as small hard shelled nuts that grew along rivers and were consumed by the Indians. Pecans were small compared with Persian walnuts which were well known in Spain. Cabeza de Vaca wrote about pecans during the period of his six year captivity (1529-1535) by Indians. Other references by Spanish explorers indicate that pecans were a major food source.

The name "pecan" is thought to have originated from the Algonquin Indian tribe word "pakan," which means a hard shelled nut that requires a stone for cracking. History also references Jean Penicault as recording the name in the early 1700's. Penicault, a ship carpenter, records the Natchez Indian village natives referencing small hard shelled nuts as "pecanes." The French in Louisiana later referenced the nut as "pecane." In French, the ending "e" indicated that the last syllable was accented. The "e" was later dropped, yielding *pecan* as we know it today.

By the mid 1700's, American Indians had apparently distributed pecans eastward to the Atlantic Ocean and southeastward to Alabama, Georgia, and Florida. Nuts were planted probably both on purpose and by accident. Many of these trees and their offspring still stand.

It is reported that George Washington and Thomas Jefferson were both fanciers of pecans. A reference in Washington's diary also mentioned planting pecans. In spite of this interest in pecans by famous Americans, pecans were scarcely mentioned in horticultural history from the late 1700's to around 1880. Early orchards (1870-1900) were typically planted from seedling trees, derived from select nuts planted in place. Ocean Springs, Mississippi, and surrounding areas had as its residents many famous pecan pioneers. W. R. Stuart, C. Forkert, T. P. Delmas, Charles E. Pabst, and others made significant contributions to commercial pecan industry development. We recognize Stuart (the most widely planted cultivar) and other pecan cultivars that were named for these important individuals. E. E. Risien, San Saba County, Texas, noticed that seedlings from planted San Saba nuts did not produce nuts like the parent. One of the resulting seedlings (of about 400) did result in the Western Schley (known as Western today). Western is the primary cultivar used in the western USA, and is still propagated widely.

Pecans developed into a valuable commercial crop in many of the native states, and were successfully transplanted to other southern states, including Georgia, Alabama, and Florida. These states are now leading producers of pecans. Other historical milestones are referenced in other facets of this book. For example, the "Pecan Varieties" chapter describes the advent of pecan breeding and genetics. This effort certainly deserves a prominent place in pecan history.

Fact or fairy tale?

Many tales exist about the properties of pecan trees, the pecans produced, and ideas on how to care for them (trees and nuts). My book delves into some of these conceptions and misconceptions in detail. I'll list a few of the more important ones below.

- Planting some pecan trees can either send your child to college or send you to the poor house – depending on your level of care and knowledge.
- The tree that grows from a planted nut will **not** produce a nut that is identical to the one planted.
- "Hardy" pecans advertised by some nurseries are typically seedling pecan trees. Typically they are grown from hardy northern pecans. As with other seedling pecans, tree and nut properties cannot be accurately predicted ahead of time.
- Pecan scions can only be successfully grafted to pecan and hickory rootstock. Pecan grafts to walnut and ash will not work.
- Overcrowding and overshading is a common cause of poor tree performance.
- Pecan trees are typically alternate bearing.
- White grubs and small round holes in pecans are signs of pecan weevil infestation. Pecan weevils usually emerge in the August to September timeframe.

- Cold-hardy pecan trees require both a cold-hardy rootstock and a cold-hardy grafted cultivar top.

I'm sure you've heard both sides of the above statements. Whether you take my word as truth is up to you.

Chapter 4
PECAN — THE TREE

When many people hear the word "pecan," they automatically think of the pecan nut— some may even picture the good things made from pecans such as pies, cookies, etc. This chapter deals with pecan, the tree. To do the best job of producing pecan nuts, it is important to understand the different tree components, including roots, trunk, branches, leaves, fluids (sap), flowers, and fruits. Like most organisms, a pecan tree's first priority is to survive. Improper management of the tree and it's environment will likely lead to few pecan nuts with poor quality. By understanding the different tree components and systems, growers and homeowners can better optimize their time, efforts, and hopefully nut production and profits.

Pecan trees are the largest members of the hickory family, often reaching a height of 75 feet or more, and the canopy spread often exceeds the height. The dense green canopy contributes to the use of pecan as a yard tree, and under the right conditions turns a beautiful shade of yellow in the fall. Although pecan is not an important lumber tree, it is sometimes used for furniture, flooring, and paneling. Pecan makes some of the best wood for smoking meats.

Tree characteristics include the following:

Root system. Pecan has a taproot oriented root system which provides a good anchoring system for the large and heavy canopy. Lateral roots develop along the length of the taproot, and often extend well beyond the canopy drip line. Feeder roots are small versions of the lateral roots, and provide most of the moisture and nutrients for the tree.

Feeder roots are fragile, and are constantly dying back and regenerate as the soil conditions change. Adventive or adventitious roots sometimes arise from the cambium layer. These roots often form from a tree injury, or when the surface position changes due to flood or other circumstances.

Trunks, branches, and shoots. The trunk is the main support for lateral branches that form the canopy. The trunk should be trained to be free of branches for a height of 6 ft. or more, depending on equipment used to maintain the orchard or yard floor. The tree structure recommended is a central leader for strength and ease of harvest. Branches should be pruned to minimize overlap, and provide adequate sunlight to central portions of the canopy. Shoots are current year leaf bearing growth. Shoot development is a good barometer for tree health. Mature growing trees should put on at least four inches of growth annually. Healthy young trees grow more rapidly, often extending new growth for a foot or more.

Buds. Buds are basically compressed versions of branches, leaves, and flowers. Terminal buds form on the end of shoots when growth stops. Lateral buds form on the sides of shoots during shoot elongation. Lateral buds usually form in clusters (or groups) of three, although sometimes four or more buds per cluster are observed. The uppermost bud in a cluster, usually the largest, is called the primary bud. The other buds are designated as reserve buds. In pecan, bud break is usually later than in other trees, minimizing susceptibility to late spring freezes.

Flowers. Pecan is *monoecious*, indicating that both male and female (pistillate) flowers are borne on the same tree. Pecan is also generally dichogamous, indicating that that the female flowers are not receptive when the staminate (male) flowers on the same tree shed pollen. The degree of dichogamy varies from cultivar to cultivar. Some trees have more overlap of pollen shed and pistillate flower receptivity than others. Pecan flowering is often referred to as "Type I" (protandrous) and "Type II" (protogynous). Protandrous varieties of pecan shed pollen before their pistillate flowers are receptive. Protogynous varieties shed pollen after their pistillate flowers are receptive. Generally speaking, it's good to have both flowering types in proximity to each other. Pistillate flowers are borne on the ends of current year growth. Staminate flowers, or catkins as they're sometimes called, are borne along the extent of one year old growth.

Nuts and fruiting

The pecan fruit is the nut plus the shuck. Pecan requires a relatively long growing season to mature its fruits. A pecan with an average nut maturity requires about 155 days from successful pollination, Of course, some of the "ultra-northern" varieties, such as 'Martzahn' require about a month less. On the other side of the coin, late varieties, such as 'Houma' require up to a month more.

Characteristics deemed desirable for in-shell pecan include:

1. Shell should be thin and brittle, but not so thin that it cracks during harvest.
2. Percent kernel should exceed 50%.
3. Packing material should separate cleanly from the kernel.
4. Nut size should be large enough to please the consumer. Size and shape preference varies with geographical location and consumer preference.
5. Shape should be oblong instead of round to align properly in mechanical cracking equipment.

Characteristics for kernels include:

1. Bright and straw colored kernels are best. Consumers relate a dark amber color to a lack of freshness.
2. Kernels should be free of fuzz.
3. Wide dorsal and ventral grooves are preferred to minimize imbedded packing material.
4. Varieties that yield a high percentage of perfect kernel halves provide added value and customer appeal.

Chapter 5

GETTING STARTED

Whether you're planting one tree or a thousand, there are right ways and wrong ways to start out. If you live in native pecan country and have a bunch of pecan trees on your farm, there are ways to improve the productivity of these pecan trees that are already in place. This chapter outlines the steps that are necessary to become one of a select breed of pecan growers. A warning! Pecan growing can become addictive. You may find yourself awake at night planning orchard layouts, or dreaming about a perfect pecan variety that accidentally grew from a nut seed from your orchard. You're almost sure to be late for dinner, and find that the sun always goes down an hour later in the orchard, compared to where your spouse is. And it always gets dark just when you are starting something critical, and critical things can usually be done by moonlight.

Looking Back

As I look back to 1980 when I first really started learning about pecans and their culture, I wonder how I could have been so uninformed. As I look back even further to 1968 when I planted the first pecan tree in my yard here in Oklahoma, I quickly figured out why I was so dumb back in 1980. Perhaps the main reason was a facade of thinking I knew more than I did; a secondary reason was not asking questions to the right people. A third reason was that after I learned to ask the right people, I didn't pay enough attention to what they told me.

Maybe that lack of knowledge was what they called the innocence of youth. Next to personal experience, learning from the experience of others is a suitable alternative. Getting older has at least taught me something.

Back to my first pecan yard tree in Oklahoma. Outside of my experience with the native pecan trees when I lived in Amarillo, I knew almost nothing about pecan varieties. Overhearing a neighbor talking about his Stuart tree, I figured

Stuart was the tree to get. A trip to the nursery netted me one Stuart tree. The nurseryman asked if I was sure I wanted a Stuart. Like a dummy, I said yes instead of asking him if he had any other suggestions. I followed the instructions on the tree for planting, and the tree lived and prospered. It had a few pecans the tenth year after planting, but they froze in the shuck. The next year, we moved to a new location just in time to see the shuck split on 37 Stuart nuts. If I had planted a Peruque or some other more precocious and early ripening cultivar, I would have put more pecans in the pantry. Looking back at the memories from 1980, I think of all the things I would do different in the ways of pecan culture if I knew in 1980 what I know today.

Like many things, getting started into pecan culture is more interesting than reading about it. I started building my pecan operation with two different approaches. One approach was by grafting improved varieties onto native root stock that grew wild on my land. Not a bad idea! Some of the grafts prospered, and I learned quickly that pecans don't grow when grafted onto ash rootstock. It didn't take long to learn to distinguish pecan from ash and walnut.

I also bought about 20 improved variety pecan trees to plant in open areas. Twelve were northern cultivars, four were Mohawk trees, and four were Maramec trees. One objective was to establish a local source of graftwood. The only water on the place was in Pecan Creek. To water the newly planted trees, extracting water out of the creek with a pump hooked to my old Ford 9N tractor seemed like a good idea. The tractor broke down shortly thereafter. After I got the tractor fixed, the creek almost ran dry. The next approach was to haul water from a neighbor's house until I broke down. It was one of the driest summers on record. My 20 planted bare root trees perished except for four that sprouted from below the grafts. If 1980 were today, I'd put in the well before I planted bare root trees. Come to think of it, I probably wouldn't plant bare root improved variety trees at all.

Every cloud does have at least a partial silver lining though. The four surviving rootstock are now big healthy improved variety trees. I chalked up the inordinate expense of my very limited success as a learning experience. The surviving rootstock were grafted about two years after they sprouted new native tops. Luckily, they were from the northern varieties which were propagated onto northern rootstock — and they were evidently tougher than the other 16 that totally perished.

A second thing I would do different is to plan the area to eventually be an orchard with regularly spaced rows. I would continue to convert native trees to improved varieties, and move appropriate ones into rows. Some of the converted natives would remain as randomly spaced temporary trees. With some luck, a few trees would be in the right places to start with. Trees in rows are much easier to care for.

I'm now experimenting with container grown rootstock from known open pollinated seed. This way, I can start with rootstock that have at least some known characteristics. Although native rootstock that grow naturally from nuts in the area are generally tolerant to cold conditions, some are better than others.

There are lots of other things that I'd do differently, but that's what this book is all about. Maybe my mistakes will help the readers of this book not to make the same ones. After all, learning from the experiences of others is a sign of intelligence, and pecan growers are a naturally smart bunch of people.

Getting Started In General

Step 1 — Get to know your County Agricultural Extension Agent.

If I could recommend only one thing for folks that live in the USA, this would be my advice. The best thing next to knowing what needs to be done is to know someone who does. County Agents have access to valuable research and to specialists in all facets of pecan culture. If they can't answer your questions, they usually know who can. Phone numbers are typically listed under County Government. They are affiliated

with the different State Land Grant Universities, and information can be obtained from this source as well.

Plan Before Purchase

A general inclination is to buy a pecan tree or even a bunch of pecan trees and then decide what to do with them. I've seen bare root pecan trees sit around for a month or two because the site wasn't ready for planting. It never fails that the weather goes to pot on these occasions, further delaying things. I've seen people with trees to plant that hit solid rock sixteen inches down. That last few inches of digging in solid rock is murder.

Even though the itch to buy trees is hard to overcome, it's best to plan your orchard layout ahead of time. Even if you're planting one or two trees in the yard, decide where they're going to be placed before you buy the trees.

Site Evaluation

If you are selecting a site for an orchard on ground that you own, pick the best site available. The list below indicates some things to consider.

1. Proper soils – Pecans prefer deep alluvial soils that are found along creeks and river bottoms. Some deep upland soils are also suitable, but usually require additional preparation and more intense management.

2. Proper drainage – Soils must have good drainage. Standing water for long periods, or soils that are too wet, will deprive the trees of oxygen and the ability to absorb nutrients.

3. Good air flow – Air movement through the orchard minimizes disease development such as scab.

4. Adequate soil moisture retention.

5. Irrigable lands – If the orchard is to be irrigated, the land must be relatively flat. Consult an irrigation specialist for a second opinion.

6. A stable water table that varies from about 8 feet to 20 feet.

7. Flooding – Floods can wash away most of the pecan crop, and subject pecan trees to moisture stress.

The chapter on **"Nutrition and Water Requirements"** contains supplemental information on these topics.

Site Preparation for Orchards

Proper preparation of the orchard site can eliminate a lot of problems later on. Some site problems can be overcome with preparation; some cannot. Cost is usually the determining factor. Preparation steps include the following:

1. Clear the land and kill out any permanent weeds, such as Johnson grass, especially within the row areas where the trees are to be planted. This is best accomplished the year before with a post emergence herbicide labeled for use on the problem weeds.
2. Make adjustments to the surface, such as leveling, providing drainage, etc.
3. Clear adjoining lands as best as possible to improve air movement, and minimize pest habitat.
4. Prepare the soil with deep cultivation, especially along rows where trees are to be planted.
5. Adjust soil nutrients (with the exception of nitrogen) and pH to acceptable levels.

Other Things to Consider

Spacing – Remember that pecan trees grow to be big – typically reaching a height and spread of 80 feet. Spacing of 30 feet between trees is a minimum. Even if spaced at thirty feet, thinning will be necessary in the future. This means cutting down a tree or two in the yard or several trees in the orchard. Overcrowding is a major cause for poor performance in pecan trees.

Soil Suitability – It's best to determine if the soil is suitable for pecans before planting. If soil is shallow, it's probably best to grow something else. A soil test may be a worthwhile investment both for yard and orchard environments. Your County Agricultural Extension Agent can usually provide you procedures for doing this. If soils

are lacking in certain critical nutrients such as phosphorus, or if the soil pH is out of an acceptable range, corrective measures are most easily accomplished before trees are planted. Generally speaking, nutrient deficiencies other than nitrogen should be treated before trees are planted. See the references for soil testing and soil additives (fertilizers and pH control) in the **"Nutrition and Water Requirements"** chapter.

Water – Be sure that an adequate source of water is present before planting new trees – especially bare root pecans. Container grown trees are more tolerant to a lack of timely moisture than bare root trees. Survival percentages and growth will be better for both bare root and container grown trees if water can be supplied at the correct times and in the right amounts. In areas where pecans must be irrigated, plan the system before planting the trees.

Weeds and grass – Tough weeds such as Johnson grass, brush, poison ivy, etc. should be eliminated before trees are planted. Also, thick and tall turf is tough competition for young pecan trees. I saw a five acre orchard planted with one year old bare root trees. The trees were planted in an existing bluestem grass hay meadow. After a month the trees were totally hidden. At the end of the year, about 10 trees out of over 200 survived. It is best to establish and maintain a zone of bare ground about 3 to 5 feet wide on either side of newly planted trees. Of course this is more easily initiated before the trees are planted. A follow-up treatment after planting with a preemergence herbicide labeled for newly planted trees will help keep the row areas free of weeds. The width of the bare ground strip can be enlarged as the trees grow. Sod "middles" can be left intact to minimize mud and other management problems.

Acquiring & Planting Trees

There are several ways to acquire trees, depending on how much money you have to spend, how much time you have, and where you live. Time required is usually inversely proportional to initial cost.

Importance of Rootstock

In my opinion, the type of rootstock is about as important as the cultivar propagated onto the rootstock. Improved variety pecan trees such as Colby, Wichita, Pawnee, and many others are obtained by grafting or budding seedling pecan trees with buds or scions from the respective named varieties. In many cases the nursery that sells the trees is unable to tell the source of the rootstock. Many wholesale nursery growers will select rootstock based on their growth performance as opposed to other attributes such as tolerance to cold weather. Rootstock that grow rapidly to a size that can be grafted are more profitable to the nursery than rootstock that grow more slowly. Whole orchards have been lost due to improper rootstock selection when extremely cold weather or sharp drops in temperature are encountered. It is usually good practice not to move pecan rootstock seeds more than 200 miles north of their native location. Pollinating pistillate flowers from southern varieties with pollen from northern cultivars, and vice versa, is not recommended. (Personal communication, L. J. Grauke, USDA-ARS Pecan Breeding and Genetics Worksite, College Station, Texas.)

Southern rootstock —Nuts from open pollinated flowers of Apache, Riverside, and Burkett cultivars are examples of growthy southern rootstock that are popular in the southwestern USA. Elliott, Curtis, and Moore are popular rootstock for the southeastern USA. Although these rootstock are acceptable in southern areas where pecans are grown, unfortunately they generally lack freeze resistance requirements for the more northerly pecan regions. Northern rootstock are a poor choice for southern regions, since trees from northern rootstock will typically have a slower rate of growth – thus less production in the early years than their southern counterparts.

Northern rootstock – Giles, Colby, Lucas, and other northern cultivars make the best rootstock for the cold weather conditions that are prevalent in the more northerly parts of the pecan belt. Native pecans from these northerly regions generally make acceptable rootstock, although their performance is more variable. Although southern rootstock grow faster than those from the north, a dead tree that froze out doesn't grow at all.

Trees for the Yard

The easiest way to acquire a tree for the yard is to buy a container grown or bare root improved variety tree from a reliable nursery. Select a cultivar that is suited for your area, as described in the **"Pecan Varieties"** chapter. If possible, determine the source of the rootstock. I've seen lots of "bargain" trees here in Ponca City that froze to the ground in 1991, 1989, and other years that had harsh winters and early freezes. In Ponca City, trees such as the Mahan variety may produce nuts that fail to fully mature or freeze in the shuck two years out of three.

Also, pick a cultivar that has a good tree structure and is as resistant as possible to diseases such as scab. Pollination is also a factor to be reckoned with if you want to gather nuts from your trees, since pecan is generally not self pollinating. In areas where other pecan trees are scarce, plant at least two varieties that shed pollen at the right time. See the cultivar descriptions and chart on flowering in the **"Pecan Varieties"** chapter. If you have an interest in horticulture and want to take the time and effort, the other methods for acquiring trees will work just fine.

Trees for the Orchard

An orchard is generally thought of as a regularly spaced planting of 20 trees or more. One major difference between a few trees in the yard and a bunch of trees in the orchard is the equipment required to keep them going.

My preferred method is to start trees from known seed in containers, and move the one year seedlings to the orchard in the late fall. After the trees are established for two or more years, graft them via a four-flap or other technique to the desired cultivars.

Buying and Planting Bare Root Improved Variety Trees. First of all, pick a reliable source for your tree purchases. Bargain trees are not a bargain in the long run. I've personally observed purchased trees that were not true to variety.

Some were even seedling trees that were labeled as well known cultivars. Most of the time it is possible to tell a grafted tree from a seedling early-on, but not always. After the time and trouble invested in the five to ten years that it takes to produce a few pecans, it is tough to see nuts that are the wrong kind. Check the tree for freeze or other damage. A live tree will have green under the bark when lightly nicked. Dig a hole that is as deep as the root is long after the root has been pruned. The tap root end should rest on the bottom of the hole.

Root pruning – An average bare root pecan tree typically has a tap root 30 or more inches long. Contrary to what seems to be logical, bare root trees do better if the tap root is pruned back to a length of about eighteen inches. Root pruning encourages the development of lateral roots along the taproot. It's also easier to dig a twenty inch hole than one that is three feet deep. All broken and damaged lateral root parts should be removed.

Top pruning – It's best to prune the top back about 50%. Top pruning encourages more uniform budbreak, and significantly better and healthier shoot development.

Into the ground – Now it's the time you've been waiting for. It's late winter and the trees to be planted are dormant. Bare root trees must be planted while in a dormant state to maximize the chance of survival. I assume that you've kept the roots moist all this time. Put the tree centered in the hole. The tree should be planted at the same depth as it was in the nursery. Tamp the soil, then water thoroughly to remove air pockets. This is sometimes called **"watering-in"** the tree. Be prepared to give the trees an optimum dose of water about every week except when it rains, and rains enough.

Planting Small Bare Root Seedling Trees

General planting instructions are generally the same. Root and top pruning of one year old seedlings is usually not necessary. Due to several factors, survival rates for one year bare root trees planted in place in the field are usually marginal.

Planting Container Grown Trees

Container trees are generally bothered less by transplanting shock than bare root trees. Survival percentages are generally higher with container grown stock. Container grown trees are usually more tolerant to variations in water supply, although they will need regular water applications during the first year or until a permanent root system is established. Container trees can be planted over a longer calendar period than bare root trees, but it's still best to plant them while they're dormant. In other respects, container trees can be either good or bad, depending on containers and growing conditions. Don't be fooled by bare root trees that are stuck in a container and sold as container grown trees the same year. Trees of this type will usually lose all the soil when removed from the container. A common problem with older container grown trees is a twirled taproot. This usually happens with improper containers that are too shallow for the root system.

Planting container grown trees is similar to planting bare root trees. Remove damaged root ends. If the tap root is twirled, try to straighten it, or cut off most of the curled portion. Again, it's best not to purchase trees that have severely twirled taproots. Cover the top of the root ball with an inch or so of soil to minimize drying and wick action. As with bare root trees, keep the roots moist until they're in the hole and covered up. Water-in the trees.

One year old container grown seedling trees, if you can find them, are an effective and economical way to start an orchard. Be sure to check on the source of the seeds to see if they will make suitable rootstock. The trees can be grafted to improved varieties usually by the third year.

Starting Pecan Trees From Seed

Like other ways to get into the pecan business, starting from seed has its advantages and disadvantages. On the positive side, starting from seed provides:

1. Direct control of rootstock variety.
2. Low initial cost.

3. Control during the early years of the pecan tree's life.

4. Trees that lack vigor can be culled during the first year. Due to variable pollinizers and other factors, growth rates and caliper size can vary considerably even among seedlings from nuts off of the same tree. For example, nuts that developed via self pollination may lack vigor.

Now for the negative side:

1. Starting from seeds requires a considerable amount of personal time to prepare the seeds and care for the seedlings.

2. It can take up to three years to get a tree that's big enough to graft, thus delaying the time between initial planting and production compared with other options.

Steps required for growing trees from seed:

1. Select seed of the desired variety or appropriate native nuts. Choose large, well filled specimens from the current crop.

2. Soak the seed for approximately 48 hours. Change the water every twelve hours, or better yet, aerate the water with an aquarium pump or other device. This step helps to provide adequate oxygen for the nuts.

3. Layer the nuts in moist (not wet) growing media, vermiculite, or sand. Place the layered nuts in a sealed container such as a plastic bucket and store under refrigeration (approximately 40 degrees) for two to three months. This process is called stratification. If refrigerator space is a problem, the container of stratified nuts can be placed into the ground and left there in the winter. This comes closer to the natural stratification of nuts that fall from the tree and get covered up, or get buried by squirrels. Stratification should be initiated two to three months prior to planting time in the spring. Check the stratified nuts periodically to ensure that they don't dry out. Stratification enhances prompt germination and contributes to tree vigor.

4. Plant the nuts after danger of serious frost has passed. Nuts should be planted about two to three inches deep. I prefer to plant the nuts in containers instead of directly in their permanent locations. Container grown trees are easier to water, fertilize, and care for in general. Nuts planted in the ground are more susceptible to damage from squirrels, mice, and other rodents, although these varmints can munch on container planted nuts as well. Nothing is more discouraging than to find that a varmint has progressed down the row, digging up the new seedlings and eating the nuts out of the middle. Take it from someone who knows.

5. Container grown trees dry out quickly, so an automatic watering system of some sort is essential. Going without water for even a day or two can kill the trees. I water the plants for about 30 minutes per day.

6. Monthly fertilization with a slow release balanced fertilizer will improve growth rates and tree vigor. Trace elements, especially zinc, are also essential.

7. During the fall (October and November for most areas), plant the seedlings in the orchard. If the seedlings are to be kept in pots until the next growing season, winterizing is required in cold climates.

Shortcuts to Stratification

I've had reasonable success planting unstratified nuts by first soaking them in water for a couple of days. Change the water once or twice a day. Again, start with current year nuts that have been kept cold most of the time since harvest. Nuts prepared this way usually produce less vigorous seedlings than those produced from stratified seed.

Containers

Several forms of containers are suitable for starting pecan trees. I've found that containers provided by **Stuewe & Sons, Inc.**, Corvallis, Oregon, to be suitable and cost effective for growing pecans. Stuewe and Sons can be reached at **(800) 553-5331**.

Their one gallon pot (~4"*14") will easily accommodate trees through the first year and sometimes into the second.

Air Pruning

Air pruning is a process that accomplishes root pruning by exposure of growing root ends to air. Pots for air pruning typically have bottoms that are mostly open, so that roots that reach the bottom of the pots will be exposed to air and thus not elongate any further. Air pruning helps to develop a sturdy and compact root system and minimizes the twisting or twirling of taproots. If pots are left on the ground, taproots and other roots will go past the bottom of the pot and into the ground.

The First Growing Season

By June, planting success rates can be determined with reasonable accuracy. The best trees will have put on a few inches of growth. Tiny one year old seedlings will probably have grown at least an inch or two. There may be a few slow starters that haven't done much but are still alive. The first growing season after planting is both exciting and critical. All your planting efforts can go out the window if trees are not carefully maintained during this first period of growth. Following is a list of things that are required after the trees are planted to ensure the best first year survival rates and optimum growth. Most of these items apply to trees of all sizes and types.

1. Water the trees thoroughly once a week at least through September, except when a rain storm does it for you. Try not to let the trees become stressed.

2. Maintain the ground around the trees as weed free as possible.

3. Watch for insect damage and spray the trees accordingly.

4. If the trees exhibit good growth, apply nitrogen fertilizer about three times during the active growing season up until the middle of July. Use about a half cup for every inch of stem diameter per application. One year seedlings are not very big, but should receive a proportionate amount. Too much fertilizer can also cause problems such as nitrogen scorch. The fertilizer should be spread over the current root zone and a little beyond. Do not fertilize trees that are growing slowly.

5. Apply foliar zinc about every two weeks from bud break until the first of August.

The First Dormant Season

Frost is on the pumpkin, and the leaves have fallen from your fledgling pecan trees. It's surprising to see how small they look without their foliage. The dormant season is bliss in some ways, because it means that the work may slow down. If you're a workaholic, maybe this is bad news. For me, I look forward to each season, and backward thinking how glad I am that the current one is over. Pruning can be done at this time. Towards spring, inspect your central leaders and cut back any dead or damaged tips. Long and spindly growth is best cut back also. This action will help to encourage uniform budbreak in the spring.

Equipment Required

For young orchards, especially small ones, not a lot is needed in the way of special equipment. A good set of pruning shears and a back pack sprayer will suffice for a few years. Needs are dictated by the amount of time you have to spend caring for the trees, and how much money you can invest in your newfound or old interest.

A tractor is handy for several things. It can supply both the mobility and power for spray equipment. A tractor can be of help in digging the holes for trees, and for providing leveling and cultivation. Some people that find a golf cart or ATV helpful to minimize foot travel.

Later. If you can manage, get a tractor that can suffice for the bigger jobs such as shaking trees when they get too big to harvest from the ground. I wish I had bought a bigger tractor when I started my pecan operation.

Improving Native Groves

In many areas, native pecan trees are not managed for pecan production. Pecan trees are often crowded by other tree species. Brush and vines make harvest difficult, and also compete for nutrients and water. Except in bumper years, these pecans are not economical to harvest.

Production can be enhanced several fold by clearing the brush and vines, and eliminating all non-pecan trees. Removal of big trees should be done in stages to minimize sun scald and excessive wind breakage to the pecan trees that remain. A second stage of thinning pecan trees that are too close together will provide additional harvestable pecans. Overcrowding is probably the number one impediment to pecan production in native groves. Branches of one pecan tree should not touch or overlap the branches of another. In fact, spacing that gives five to ten feet of open area between the tree canopies is best.

After a grove consists mostly of pecan trees and the grove floor is manageable, supplemental fertilizer, including zinc, will further enhance yield and nut quality. Legumes and other cover crops planted around big trees will help in several ways. Besides providing nitrogen, cover crops help to encourage beneficial insects to hang around the orchard. Where flooding is a problem, cover crops will help to control erosion.

Most native groves have built in insect problems, since pecans have been present almost forever in these areas. Likewise, pecan weevils, shuckworms, and pecan nut casebearers have been around almost forever. Thus, insect and disease control is next on the agenda.

Cattle and pecans grown together can be a profitable operation. Replacing vines and brush with pasture crops can help the pecans and feed cattle at the same time. An ideal pasture crop for the orchard should contribute to soil quality by supplying nitrogen. Converting an overgrown area to suitable pecan habitat can be a rewarding experience. The results can be pleasing to the eye, and the joy of increased quality pecan production is beyond words, at least to a pecan person.

Chapter 6

ONGOING MANAGEMENT

"Man works from sun to sun, but a pecan grower's work is never done." There is some truth in my misquote. I think I once heard someone say, **"plant a pecan tree and it will grow forever without much care and attention."** It may grow all right, but the results will be disappointing to even the most tolerant of people. Managing pecan trees that can be looked upon with pride rather than dismay takes work — and a lot of it. Care in the first five or so "formative" years is especially critical. Trees are molded to provide enhanced strength and production.

Basics and Philosophies

After trees in the yard and orchard are over transplanting shock and have sunk their roots into home base, their care becomes a sort of a variable routine. Many of the same things are repeated from year to year; other things are done less frequently. Timing for these treatments depends on seasonal variation and other factors.

Training of trees is often ignored by the novice pecan grower. I guess it's a natural thing to ignore, since trees grow wild and end up looking pretty decent. Training is especially necessary for grafted trees, since the process of vegetative propagation disrupts the normal tree development process. Certain tree characteristics provide for easier care, and allow the tree to withstand heavy crop loads. Tree training is an important function and is somewhat independent of other management functions, so it is covered in this chapter.

Training in the Formative Years

As mentioned in the beginning of this book, training can be one of the time consuming processes where "good enough" usually wins out over perfection.

The Second Growing Season

The **"Getting Started"** chapter left off at the end of the first dormant season. Hopefully you are now observing budbreak on all the newly planted trees after their first winter. Realistically, there may be a few that didn't make it and weren't diagnosed in time to make replacements. There is still a possibility of using container grown trees to fill in the gaps – but that's your decision.

I'm probably more prone than a lot of people to do a bare minimum of pruning and training in the first year. If there was an obvious problem, I will probably have corrected it. My main goal though was to get a good root system started. All leaves and branches contribute to this goal whether they're in the right place or the wrong place.

Now it's time to get serious about training your trees if you haven't started already. The central leader system is recognized almost everywhere as the preferred tree structure for pecans. In simple terms, a central leader structure has one main trunk that goes from the ground to the top of the tree. Lateral branches of a smaller size radiate from this central trunk. A preferred distance between major lateral branches is approximately two feet.

The Central leader – Prominence of the central leader should be maintained. It should dominate the height of all other branches by 12 - 16 inches.

Lateral Branches – Most lateral branches are probably too low on the tree to be considered as permanent. Anything that is so low that it might get contaminated with regular herbicide treatment should be removed. Others should be tip pruned. See the section below on removing a branch. An existing lateral branch will never get any higher on the tree than its present position.

It is time to start thinking about how high on the tree you want the first permanent lateral branch to start. I recommend at least six feet from ground level. Anything lower will impede air flow and get in the way of maintenance tasks. I've seen limbs jump right down and knock people off their tractors when the unsuspecting individuals are looking in a direction opposite from the progression of their tractor. This little mishap can be deadly if the tractor runs over you. Another rule of thumb says that the first scaffold branch should be at least six inches higher than the highest point on your tractor (your head included).

The Second Dormant Season

Central Leader – Cut back the central leader to a position where the buds start to spread out. If left unpruned, closely spaced buds and the termi-

nal bud package may result in a "crow's foot" growth pattern that is difficult to correct. Any upward growing branches that compete with the central leader should be removed or cut back to provide the 12 to 16 inch prominence recommended earlier.

Lateral Branches – Remove or cut back any lateral branches that are below the first permanent lateral branch. If selection is required, choose the branch that has the widest crotch angle – up to about 60 degrees. Reject downward growing branches because they become a nuisance later on.

The Years That Follow

By this time you'll have gotten the hang of what a properly structured tree is supposed to look like. You will have seen the tree's reaction to your attempts to make it develop in ways other than its natural inclination. Different trees call for slightly different training strategies. Continue the selective process of guiding the central leader and choosing the best limbs for scaffold branches. Remember the wide angle rule and the downward growing rule. Remember also that structural problems are best corrected early instead of late in the life of a tree. I own enough weak-crotched trees to know I should have followed my own advice a little better. Of course I could lie and say that I wanted lots of examples of what not to do for my book. Secondary branches can be removed if they interfere with the tree's structure and appearance in your way of thinking. After all, these are your trees. Pecan beauty is also in the eyes of the beholder.

At some time, you will run out of patience and reach. Hopefully by then your trees will be well trained, strong and sturdy individuals that can withstand the winds, ice, and crop loads of the future.

Non-Central Leader Training

In my travels around pecan country, I've seen a lot of pecan trees that were not central leader trained. The reasons for this phenomenon are many. First of all, many pecan varieties rebel at being central leader trained. Secondly, central leader training is lots of work. Again in the formative 4 or 5 years, central leader training is manageable, and it helps to initiate a strong tree. Later, other priorities often take precedence over training.

A reasonable alternative is to watch each tree for problems, including narrow crotches, and weak forks. If these problems show up, take corrective action early-on. Also prune the lateral branches so that their spacing is what you want. Eighteen to twenty four inches apart is not a bad selection. Selected branches should give the tree a well balanced appearance.

This is also a reasonable approach if you are managing trees started by someone else. Remember to be expedient in correcting tree structural problems. Wind and ice are non-selective pruners. These natural factors seem to prefer a split down the middle over removal of one single branch or another.

Removing a Branch

There are good ways, bad ways, safe ways, and dangerous ways to remove a branch. The bigger the branch, the greater the concern. Cutting off a branch is a sure way to pinch a saw (hand or the power variety) if it is done incorrectly. I don't plan on giving recommendations. Just read up on the process if you lack experience in tree surgery. What I will tell you is where to cut the branch. A common mistake is to cut the branch off too closely to where it's attached. Another common mistake is to cut it off too far away from the parent branch, leaving a troublesome stub. Just right is just right.

As a branch grows, it forms a sort of separation from the parent branch. A ring or ridge of dense wood forms the separation and is called a branch collar. As a branch enlarges, the collar produces a chemical barrier that inhibits invading organisms from entering the tree. Thus pruning cuts should leave the branch collar intact. A proper pruning cut should leave a circular cross section after the cut has been made. If the cross section pattern is vertically oblong, you have probably cut too deeply. Some say that tree pruning compound can help to protect the tree. Others say it won't

help. With a little experience you will learn to make the cuts properly.

Thinning and Pruning

Thinning and pruning are required from time to time to improve nut production and quality. Some pruning is usually done on an annual basis. Thinning is usually required only a few times in a lifetime.

Thinning

For most family operated pecan projects, thinning can be a tough pill to swallow. People get attached to trees; at least I do. Pecan trees are usually in place long enough to sort of develop a personality. Each tree has with it a sequence of memories. My wife might say, "That's the first tree our cat climbed to get away from the neighbor's dog. Surely you aren't thinking about cutting it down." Seems like I remember that the cat went up the tree a little ways to better be in a position to jump on the dog's back. The dog took off in a hurry to escape the cat's wrath, teeth, and claws. Our son, now grown and off on his own for 20 years, might look at the big native tree with the unique trunk structure and say, "Dad, that's the tree where you promised to build a tree house for me. I'm still waiting." I know there are a few trees that are so special that I will never cut them down. Sentiment often controls events more than prudent business decisions and conformance to regular patterns. I guess that this is maybe the biggest difference between a pecan operation developed as a family project, and one that is purely for business. Now I'll try to tell you what you should do in the way of thinning, but don't use my pecan operation as an example.

As pecan trees grow, they will eventually become overcrowded. This will happen whether your trees are 25 feet apart, 50 feet apart, or so on. The need is certain; only the timing is variable. I've heard of orchards that were thinned to trees 70 feet apart, and are in need of thinning again.

Trees require sunlight to live and grow and produce nuts. There is no practical way to control the source or amount of sunlight, so the alternative is to remove trees and branches that inhibit sunlight distribution to critical tree areas. As a rule of thumb, if the trees collectively cast shade at high noon that covers more than 60 percent of the area, it's time to think of tree thinning. Another time to think of thinning is when branches of different trees start to overlap.

In an orchard, trees are often removed by selecting alternate trees along a row diagonal. In groves, yard plantings, and orchards with different cultivars, thinning is often accomplished by choosing the worst tree with the poorest nuts. Hopefully you won't be as sentimental as I am when it comes to choosing the best trees to remove.

Pruning

Pruning of mature pecan trees usually consists of cutting back or removing limbs that get in the way of maintenance functions. In other cases, selective pruning is done to improve sunlight distribution, and to eliminate weak crotches that were overlooked during earlier years. In the years that I've had my trees, the distance between ground level and the first scaffold branch has increased for various reasons. I have also strengthened tree structure by cutting away one side of a narrow crotch. Mother Nature did a little of her own pruning from time to time via strong winds and ice. It's usually good to cut away downward growing limbs that arise from lower scaffold branches. Limbs that rub or cross other limbs are candidates for removal, if they are reachable. This type of pruning helps the appearance and functionality of pecan trees. Climbing way up into large trees with saw in hand is too dangerous for my risk threshold.

Pruning to improve nut production capacity has met with mixed success. Hedging, heading back, are examples of this management practice.

A Calendar for Pecan Growers

Most pecan producing State Cooperative Extension Services publish a calendar for pecan growers. Timing for different maintenance functions varies from state to state due to seasonal and geographical variations. See your agricultural agent for recommendations for your area.

The pecan's internal calendar is more consistent. There is the dormant season, budbreak, leaf and shoot expansion, a time when growth stops, leaf drop, and so on. Nut development time varies from about 135 days to over 200 days. Calendars typically include both calendar months and identifiable pecan growth milestones to identify proper timing for the different maintenance functions.

The Dormant Season

Dormancy in pecan usually lasts through December, January, February, and into March or April when bud swell and bud break start to occur. Management during this time period consists of:

1. Complete harvesting.
2. Remove trees to meet space requirements.
3. Perform dormant season training.
4. Remove dead limbs, and other limbs that interfere with management functions.
5. Apply nitrogen fertilizer, preferably during the last month of the dormant season. Other nutrients, including micronutrients, can be applied during the entire dormant season.
6. Begin stratification of seed nuts in January or February.
7. Make any needed equipment repairs.
8. Clean up and/or burn debris such as limbs, shucks, etc.
9. Plant or move trees.
10. Read all the literature that you didn't have time for earlier.
11. Order pesticides and apply preemergence herbicide.

Budbreak Through May

This is the period of pollen shed, nut fertilization, and shoot elongation.

1. Apply phylloxera control shortly after budbreak to trees had that phylloxera last year and to adjacent trees.
2. Apply your first foliar zinc spray (if needed) when leaf area is sufficient to catch the spray.

3. If needed, apply a pre-pollination spray for scab.

4. Start bark grafts and four flap grafts when shoot expansion reaches one to two inches or more. This is usually three to four weeks after bud break. Optimum grafting season lasts approximately a month.

5. Monitor casebearer infestation and spray accordingly.

6. Apply second zinc and post-pollination scab spray if required.

7. Maintain orchard floor; apply postemergence herbicide.

June through Mid August

This is the period after pollination and is the time of nut sizing. The period of growth usually ceases by mid-July.

1. Monitor second generation casebearer levels and take any corrective action needed.

2. Conserve moisture; irrigate when needed and/or pray for rain.

3. Stake successful grafts, and conduct first stage pruning.

4. Continue scab and zinc sprays.

5. Watch for fall webworm, shuckworm, aphid outbreaks, and other insect problems. Apply appropriate control measures.

6. Set out weevil traps before August.

7. Spray for weevils only if conditions warrant control.

8. Collect leaf analysis samples in July or as recommended in your area.

9. Continue orchard floor management and apply postemergence herbicide as needed.

Mid August through September

This is the period of shell hardening, and shucksplit for early maturing cultivars.

1. This is the prime time for weevil, shuckworm, and aphid damage. Monitor and spray accordingly.

2. Prepare the ground for harvest.

3. Watch for squirrel depredation and take corrective action.

4. Plant cool season cover crops.

5. Start to harvest early ripening cultivars.

October and November

This is the period of shucksplit for medium and late maturing cultivars.

1. Complete harvest preparation.

2. Watch for late weevil problems; note pesticide restrictions regarding spray around shucksplit time.

3. Discourage crow, blue jay, and squirrel depredation the best that you know how.

4. Pray that it won't rain until harvest is over.

5. Harvest all that you can and pray that prices will exceed production costs.

Chapter 7
PECAN VARIETIES

Over a thousand pecan varieties (cultivars) have been identified and named. Of these thousand plus, approximately sixty are now recommended for propagation in two or more states across the USA. There is no perfect cultivar; especially when the different pecan producing geographic locations are considered. Natural selection and pecan breeding will continue to add cultivars to the list from which growers can select. Additional evaluation and changing conditions will also remove cultivars that are currently popular.

Named and Unnamed Pecans

Literally millions of different pecan trees can be found across the USA. Only a few of these are managed by human beings; others grow wild throughout creek and river bottoms, and other climatological areas that are conducive for pecan trees to grow. Volume I is concerned with less than fifty of these varieties. These select varieties (cultivars) have either been chosen as being the "masters of the race," or have been specially bred to accomplish certain objectives.

When a pecan pistillate flower is fertilized, matures, and sprouts to form a new tree, it becomes a new variety. You can say with almost perfect certainty that each pecan tree grown from seed will be like no other in existence. New pecan trees, like human babies, are unique individuals. With pecan trees, however, we can vegetatively propagate new ones to form exact replicates of any desired tree by grafting or using other similar techniques.

Native pecan is a term that can apply to the bulk of these millions of varieties. These are the pecans that grow naturally in a particular region – the pecans people call "natives". Mother Nature has conducted Her own selective breeding process since the beginning, yielding cultivars that survive and thrive in the local individual environments.

Seedling pecan is another term that is often used when pecans are talked about. Of course, the native pecans that we just described are seedlings. Seedlings are, in general terms, trees generated naturally by open pollination. In more specific terms, seedling pecans are usually thought of as trees derived from nuts planted by man.

Thoroughbred pecan is a name that I have selected for a third class of pecans. These are the pecans that have been produced by controlled pollination of pecan pistillate flowers, and both parents are known for sure. Man has studied pecan genetics, and has used the knowledge gained to speed the development of superior pecan cultivars for the future. Pecan cultivars produced from the USDA pecan breeding program are examples of this category.

Papershell Pecan is a term used by many. Characteristics typically include large size, and shells thin enough to be cracked in the hand.

Geographic Considerations

Pecans are usually categorized into northern and southern cultivars. Within these classes, cultivars are often distinguished as to whether they are best suited to western or to eastern regions. The major pecan producing regions are in the southern USA, Mexico, Brazil, and Australia. Other world-wide entities also have climates conducive to pecan culture.

Cold tolerance. "Northern variety" is a term that has a particular meaning in pecan country, and is described later in some detail. All other pecans can be categorized as southern cultivars. As described later in the new context of Volume II, I have defined a class of pecans called "ultra-northern" pecan.

Scab-disease resistance. Many pecan varieties are subject to significant pecan scab and other fungal diseases. These cultivars are impossible, or at best difficult, to grow economically in eastern regions. Disease prone cultivars are typically referenced as "western" varieties. Western and Wichita are examples of this category. Other varieties have better resistance to fungal diseases and are classed as "eastern" varieties. Although these more disease resistant cultivars will also survive in western regions, water requirements, maturity time, and other factors reduce their usefulness in the western areas. Representatives from all three classes (native, seedling, thoroughbred) are represented.

Older Cultivars – Several older cultivars are still considered economically viable as alternatives for new plantings. Included in this list are Desirable, Stuart, and Western. Some older cultivars such as Curtis and Elliott are still highly recommended for yard plantings. Existing orchards of other older cultivars can still be economically viable; however, problems inherent with these cultivars inhibit their consideration for new plantings. In other words, other newer cultivars are easier to manage and are more profitable – at least under current conditions. Included in this list are: Schley, Moneymaker, San Saba Improved, Van Deman, and Success. Other older cultivars are also successful under specific conditions.

Breeding Stock – Schley, Mahan, Success, Odom, and a few other older varieties were and are sometimes still utilized as breeding stock for USDA and private pecan breeding programs.

Other Recommended Cultivars – Other cultivars are currently on the lists recommended for the southeastern pecan regions. Properties such as late maturity restrict some of them from being adapted to other regions. Some cultivars such as Forkert have been "hidden away" for whatever reasons, and are now being tested in other regions. Candy, Moreland, Melrose, Owens, and Sumner are currently recommended in several southeastern states, and may be utilized later in other areas.

USDA Cultivars

The USDA Pecan Breeding and Genetics Program Headquarters is located near College Station, Texas. The original site at Brownwood is still active, and is a repository for many of the older test varieties, a block of historically significant cultivars, and NPACTS evaluation plots. NPACTS stands for the National Pecan Advanced Clone Testing System. Other NPACTS sites are managed in cooperation with state agricultural and university entities, and selected individuals.

To date, many thousands of clones have been tested, resulting in 25 cultivars released for individual and commercial plantings. Recent history indicates that more than 20,000 are evaluated for every cultivar that is released.

Cultivar References

For additional information on pecan cultivars, see:

1. Pecans - A Grower's Perspective, G. Wesley Rice, Published by PecanQuest Publications, Ponca City, Oklahoma.
2. Pecan Cultivars - Past and Present, Tommy E. Thompson and Fountain Young, published by: The Texas Pecan Growers Association, Inc., College Station, Texas.
3. Pecan Cultivars - The Orchard's Foundation, Darrell Sparks, published by: Pecan Production Innovations, Watkinsville, Georgia.
4. Pecan Production in the Southeast, published by the Alabama Cooperative Extension Service, Auburn University, Alabama.

Cultivar Properties and Recommendations

Tables and cultivar pictures/passports are included along with the new selections in Volume II. I felt that is is best to show all cultivars together in the new organizational structure. These pictures and descriptions are included in pages 52-82.

Chapter 8
PECAN PROPAGATION TECHNIQUES

Pecan trees grown from planted pecan nuts do not maintain the same tree or nut characteristics as the tree that produced the nut. The characteristics of a new tree grown from nut seed cannot be predicted ahead of time. To produce a tree with known characteristics and nut quality, vegetative propagation by grafting or budding onto a suitable pecan or hickory rootstock is required. The following descriptions outline the more common techniques and procedures for accomplishing these objectives.

General Considerations

Since pecan trees don't reproduce true from seeds, vegetative propagation is needed to ensure the production of trees that have known characteristics. Vegetative propagation is accomplished by transferring buds and connected bark from a tree that has the desired characteristics to an established "rootstock." A rootstock is the root system and a trunk portion of a tree that is compatible with the cultivar that has the desired characteristics. For pecan trees, acceptable rootstock are other pecan trees, and hickory trees. A pecan rootstock is usually preferable over a hickory rootstock since hickory typically grows at a slower rate than pecan. The transferred bud or graft forms a union with the stock and develops into a new top of the desired variety. The tree portion above the graft is of the new variety; the plant material below the point of the graft remains as it was.

Techniques for accomplishing the transfer process are called grafting and budding.

Rootstock and Propagation Wood

One requirement for propagation is a suitable rootstock that is adapted to the area where the tree is to be grown. Perhaps the most important factor to consider is tolerance to cold winters. I have seen many grafted trees grow and prosper for several years, then be killed to the ground by a severe winter. A good choice for rootstock is a tree from a native nut (seedling or named variety) from the area where the tree is to be grown. **The rootstock should be actively growing, either in place or in a suitable container.** rootstock that have recently been transplanted will usually yield few successful grafts. Other information is provided in the section on rootstock.

A second requirement is propagation wood from a tree of the variety to be propagated. The best choices are shoots from vigorous one year old wood. Two year old wood can be successfully used, but the graft will typically start growth more slowly. Wood diameter varies from approximately quarter inch to an inch. The wood should have plump buds and be free from freeze damage. Propagation wood can be collected at the proper time and stored under refrigeration until time to begin propagation. Unless you are sure of your variety and have trees with vigorous shoots, it is usually best to purchase propagation wood from a reliable source.

Technique Versus Tree Size

The **four-flap** technique is typically used for small caliper limbs and tree trunks that are up to an inch in diameter at the point of the graft.

The **bark graft** is usually applied to limbs or trunks that are from one to four inches in diameter at the point of the graft.

The **patch bud** is typically applied to small caliper limbs and trunks up to one inch in diameter. Patch budding can also be applied to larger diameter growth if some of the outer bark is shaved away. Patch budding can be performed either in the spring or in late summer.

Other techniques, including the whip graft, and cleft graft exist; however, they are typically more difficult to perform with success than those mentioned above. Patch budding, bark grafting, and four-flap techniques will accommodate virtually all tree sizes and conditions except for very small caliper nursery stock.

Other Considerations

Grafting and budding techniques described in this publication require that the bark on the stock be **"slipping."** This ensures an adequate flow of sap to the graft. Slipping bark will peel easily from the inner wood. Bark usually slips sufficiently when the leaf package (rachis plus the tip leaflet) is two or so inches long. A common mistake is to attempt grafting too early in the season.

Grafting requires that the bark on the scion be tight. Scionwood collected while dormant, and then properly refrigerated until use will have tight bark. Graftwood collected too late in the season will often start to swell its buds even under proper refrigeration. I've even unpacked some scion wood that had initiated growth — a sure sign that the wood was collected too late.

Successful propagation requires that the **cambium** layer of the scion be in direct contact with the cambium layer of the stock. The cambium is a thin layer of colorless cells between the bark and the inner wood. It is necessary to cut down to and into the inner wood of the scion to ensure exposure of the cambium layer. Bark that is peeled back from the stock usually ensures exposure of the cambium layer.

If the grafting or budding process is successful, **callus** tissue will form along the union of the stock and the scion or patch. These callus cells develop both from the stock and the transplanted tissue (scion or patch). The callus area causes an enlargement in the caliper of both the stock and scion at the point of the graft.

Buds will typically start to swell in two or three weeks if a graft is going to take, although I've seen the buds remain dormant for over a month, then start rapid growth.

Many people don't realize that the grafting or budding process generates an entire new top above the point of the graft. **The old top of the tree or limb is cut away and discarded.** This new top starts from a bud on the scion. A lady that asked me to graft a tree almost fell over with shock when I cut the top off of her beautiful four year old pecan tree. Since then, I've always told the person what I had to do before starting the stock preparation.

Topworking

Topworking is a term used when relatively large trees are converted to a new cultivar. Bark grafts are typically applied to several major limbs. Four-flap grafts are also sometimes applied to water sprouts that develop from limbs that were cut back during the previous year. Limbs and any fruit that develop below the grafts will remain the original variety. These limbs from the original variety should be removed gradually during the first two or three years of growth of the new grafts.

The bark or inlay graft (I use the two terms synonymously) is used to graft or top-work trees or limbs up to four (and sometimes larger) inches in diameter at the point of the graft. There are several variations of this technique, and many individuals have different ideas on special adaptations that improve their success.

Graftwood (Scion wood)

A typical scion is about six inches long and from about 1/4 to 1/2 inches in diameter. The scion should be free from freeze damage, showing green when the bark of the scion is scratched. It is best if the scion has at least two sets of buds. Although a single bud will do, it's good to have the insurance of a second or third bud in case one gets damaged. The buds must be alive. Live buds are green under the outer and inner bud scales. The author has graftwood available for most of the cultivars listed in this publication. Your Agricultural County Extension Agent will also usually have a list of graftwood sources.

Steps in the techniques should ensure:

1. The closest possible direct contact between the scion edges and the stock inlay cut.

2. The contact between the scion and the stock should remain solid and safe from separation.

3. The graft should be protected from excessive heat build-up and loss of moisture.

4. Steps should be taken to initiate callus development at the base of the scion.

Required Tools and Supplies

- Small bow saw or folding saw
- Hand shears
- Grafting knife or suitable alternative
- Tack hammer
- A medium duty staple gun like the JT21 and 5/16" staples
- Half to three quarter inch brads
- Green or white plastic grafting tape
- Aluminum foil
- Pint and/or quart size plastic bags
- Carpenter's apron or plastic tote to carry the tools and supplies
- (Optional) orange shellac, black pruning compound, or white school glue

---

Grafting Techniques

See pages 104-106 for further information.

Oblique Bark Graft. Although I have used the "conventional" bark graft, the "Texas Inlay Bark Graft," and other similar techniques, the Oblique Bark Graft works best for me. It requires only a single cut on the stock, and the required contact between the stock and scion is more easily achieved.

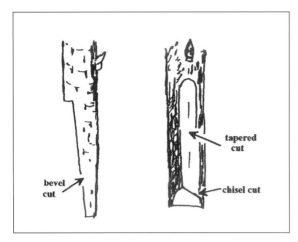

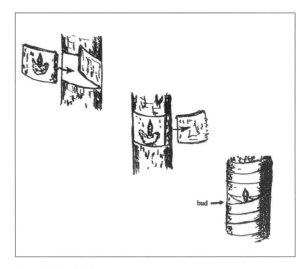

Patch bud illustrations

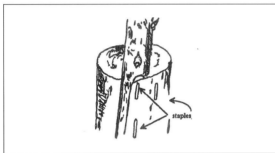

Oblique bark graft schematic

Three (or Four) Flap Graft

Four-flap grafting is used to propagate small seedling trees, and limbs from larger trees. This technique is one of the easiest to accomplish, and the resulting graft is usually strong and sturdy. The graft works best if the scion and stock are equal in size. Some variation in size between the stock and scion can be accommodated. I find it best if the scion is slightly larger than the stock rather than vice versa.

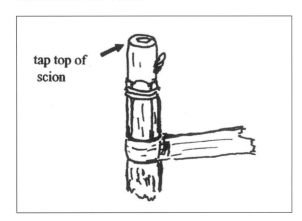

Three-flap graft schematic

General Maintenance and Aftercare of Grafted Trees

Proper aftercare of propagation efforts during the first few years is as important as the propagation procedures. Without this care, many successful grafts will die back or blow out.

Removal of Plastic Bags and Foil

Plastic bags and foil can be removed in August or September of the year that the grafting was done. If ants are working the graft, the protective coverings can be removed earlier. I have also left the coverings on all winter with no adverse results.

Pruning

1. It is very important to maintain the graft as the dominant growth on the stock. During the first summer, remove extraneous growth in the vicinity of the graft. If secondary growth is allowed to dominate, the graft will often stop growing and die back. Cut back secondary growth if it exceeds the height of the graft. Limbs below the graft can be used as "throttles" to regulate the growth of the graft. Cut back these throttle branches by about half their length each year. They can usually be cut back entirely during the winter of the third year after the propagation procedure was done. If the graft is growing too slowly, the rate of cutback can be increased.

2. As the graft develops, train the new top to a central leader. Some cultivars require more training than others. See the earlier section on tree training for further information.

3. Keep extraneous brush and other plants from growing around the newly propagated tree. Grafted trees that are excessively shaded or crowded will not develop properly. Poison ivy, small brush, and other growth can be effectively treated with ROUNDUP®. Carefully follow the directions on the product label. ROUNDUP® is a registered trademark of Monsanto Chemical Company.

4. Protect grafted trees from any livestock that use the area with fences or other barriers.

5. Tags may gradually become overwalled with bark as the tree grows. Nails holding the tags should checked every three years or so and readjusted if necessary. This completes the aftercare section.

Chapter 9
PEST AND DISEASE MANAGEMENT

Pecans are favored for consumption by humans and many other life forms. Besides seeking out the nuts, predators enjoy consuming leaves, twigs, and other parts of the pecan tree. Fungal diseases are also prevalent in many areas where pecans are grown. Successful growers and homeowners must learn to recognize these predators and diseases, and apply corrective measures when they are needed. Specific beneficial creatures are helpful in controlling their undesirable counterparts. These predacious insects and other beneficials should be recognized and encouraged. Some pests, such as the pecan weevil, can currently be controlled only through the use of chemical pesticides. Selection of the proper product and application at the proper time is essential. *Biological pesticides* have been introduced recently into the pecan management arena. These biological agents are generally harmless to beneficial insects, and effectively control several serious pecan pests.

Basic Considerations

Control of pecan pests can be accomplished in part by prudent management practices and proper cultivar selection. Recently, research has provided partial alternatives to control of pests via chemicals. Selective pesticides have allowed the pecan grower to minimize damage to important beneficial insects and other beneficial organisms. Pesticide suppliers can also be commended for their interest and concern for non-target organisms, and their efforts to ensure the safest possible product use.

Cultivar Selection

Perhaps the best initial defense for the control of many pests and diseases is to select pecan cultivars that show natural resistance to problems that are prevalent in a designated geographic area. For example, in the humid southeastern areas of the USA, Western is a very poor cultivar choice because of its susceptibility to scab. On the other hand, Western is grown very successfully in regions of the Southwest.

Much has been written on natural resistance of different cultivars to specific insect pests. When there is some physiological reason for this resistance, such as leaf texture and nut maturity date, this natural resistance may indeed be real. I have observed even in my small orchard, exceptions and contradictions to many of these stated insect resistance factors. It is my belief that many of the immunity and resistance factors are more related to timing and ecological factors than they are to specific cultivars. As with other factors, resistance of the different cultivars to insect problems varies considerably with geographical location.

Even with the best cultivar selection and management practices, pesticide use is often necessary in virtually all areas where pecans are grown. Humid areas and areas where pecans are indigenous are typically more prone to have these problems than arid regions where pecans were introduced during the last half century.

Management Practices

A key to effective control is proper timing and proper pesticide selection. Proper timing is often dependent on recognizing when and at what level the pest enters the orchard in a form that is susceptible to the control agent. Many insects over-winter or lay eggs in debris such as old nut husks, limb piles, etc. These insect habitats should be burned or destroyed in some other manner.

Disease Trees - Every orchard usually has a few trees that seem to be especially good at harboring insects and catching disease. I suppose it's like some situations with us humans. I can walk through grass that is infested with chiggers and never get a single bite. My wife can attract a chigger from a mile away. Maybe we'll never know why some trees are more susceptible to disease and insects than others. Problem trees should be considered for removal when selective thinning is conducted in the orchard.

Pesticide Basics - There are currently about 200 products registered by the federal government for use on pecans. Some old standby products such as ZOLONE® are no longer available; others will likely disappear in future years. Insecticides, herbicides, and fungicides are all being closely scrutinized for possible environmental impacts. Since the prognosis for these agents is so variable, I feel that it is more important to list sources of information for pesticides than to elaborately describe products that are available for use at this point in time.

Product Labels and Formulations

Labels for pesticide products provide key information for product use, product restrictions, susceptible pests, and other relevant data. The entire label should be read and understood before products are used. Follow all usage guidelines and instructions precisely. **As far as I know, all pesticide manufacturers will provide copies of product labels upon request.**

Most pesticide products are available in different formulations, for example – wettable powders and various suspensions. Spray equipment type and other variables dictate the best formulation to use. Consult product suppliers or your County Extension Agent if you are unsure of the best formulation. Formulation codes are often designated by a 2 or 3 character symbol following the product name, for example – *SEVIN® 80S available in 1994*.

Products, manufacturers and distributors change frequently. Although many of the chemicals that were available in 1994 are still available, they are now offered by different suppliers. See Volume II, pg 108, for a current list.

Chemical Pesticides

Chemicals fall under two specific categories when it comes to their application: general use and restricted use pesticides. This book covers the general use pesticides. A license must be obtained to apply restricted use pesticides.

Chemicals that are useful to the pecan grower can also be classified into three categories, based on the problem for which they are used. First, insecticides are used to control insects and other small bug-like critters. Second, fungicides are used to control fungal diseases such as scab. Third, herbicides are used to control undesirable vegetative growth such as annual weeds and poison ivy.

Many chemicals that were once common for control of pecan pests are now unavailable. Chemicals that are currently available for unrestricted use may some day require a license, or disappear from the marketplace altogether. With these possibilities in mind, the pecan grower should pay special attention to the sections on **Biological Insecticides** and **Natural Pest Control Methods**. These may be the major pest control alternatives in future years.

Biological Insecticides

The bacteria *Bacillus thuringiensis* or *"Bt"* as it's commonly called, is an introduction to the pecan pest control arena. It controls the larvae of many important pests, primarily lepidoptera species (moths and butterflies), and is basically harmless to most other insects and organisms.

Thus *Bt* can be sprayed onto pecan trees with little risk of damage to beneficial creatures of the pecan orchard. It is one of the safest agents for humans to apply, and *Bts* currently have no grazing or orchard reentry restrictions. Pecan nut casebearers, fall webworms, and walnut datana are damaging to the orchard in their larval form, and can often be effectively controlled with timely applications of *Bt*. While the hickory shuckworm meets the "moth larvae" criteria, its life cycle provides little opportunity for ingestion of biological or chemical agents.

Bacillus thuringiensis is a naturally occurring soil borne bacteria that is found worldwide. It is non toxic to humans, wildlife, and most non-target organisms. It is thus an excellent alternative to some of the more non-selective chemicals when one wishes to control insects that are susceptible to *Bt*. Microbial pesticides such as B*t* currently (2005) show few indications of resistance in target pests.

To be effective, *Bt* must be ingested (eaten) by the target insect. Insect larvae typically stop feeding within a few hours after ingestion, thus damage stops. The larvae die within a few days. Timing of spray programs is very important since residual effectiveness is short.

SAFETY FIRST AND ALWAYS

Always use extreme caution in handling and applying all agricultural pesticides.

- ❏ **Read and follow all the instructions on the label precisely.**
- ❏ **Use proper care in storing these agents, and dispose of containers properly.**
- ❏ **Wear recommended protective clothing.**
- ❏ **Use eye protection.**
- ❏ **Use respiration protection.**
- ❏ **Do not eat with contaminated hands.**
- ❏ **Shower, and change to clean clothing after each application.**
- ❏ **Obey grazing, reentry, and all other restrictions.**

Natural Aids to Pest Control

Some particular plant forms are especially good for attracting particular insects – both harmful and beneficial. Legumes are among the most unique plants in this respect. Besides adding nitrogen to the soil, legumes can contribute to the successful pest management of pecan trees.

Cover Crops – Some cover crops such as various clovers and vetches naturally attract desirable insects such as lady beetles, lacewings, and similar insects. Cover crops also add valuable nitrogen to the soil, reduce shredding costs, and improve water utilization. Predacious insects can be one of the most effective ways to reduce populations of the various aphid species that feed on pecan foliage.

Trap Crops – In a fashion similar to cover crops, trap crops can attract damaging insects such as stink bugs away from pecan trees. Crops such as black-eyed peas, purple hull peas, and other legumes attract leaf footed bugs and stink bugs like honey attracts bees. Trap crops, if planted at the right time, can concentrate populations and lure these bugs away from the pecan nuts. The trap crop can also be sprayed with a proper control agent to reduce populations of the undesirable insects. A possible drawback to the spray option is that it may also reduce populations of desirable insects and other organisms that have taken refuge in the trap crop.

Big Damage – Small Critters –The most damaging pests are often the most difficult to see. While evidence left by bigger creatures such as squirrels, crows, and even deer is often more visible, subtle small insects such as shuckworms and weevils often leave their calling cards too late to do any good. When the weevil larvae leave their telltale holes in the nuts, it's too late to treat the orchard. A talented naturalist can look at a squirrel track and tell its maker's age, weight, sex, and maybe even which pecan cultivar it had for dinner – but who can track a pecan weevil.

Integrated Pest Management (IPM)

Pest management has changed significantly over the past one or two decades, especially in the use of chemicals. Earlier, chemicals were often applied on a calendar basis - rather than on when the particular pests occurred in the orchard. Earlier pesticides had a relatively long residual effect; however, many of the applications lacked effectiveness due to improper timing. Also, many of the pests developed a resistance to particular pesticides, due in part to repeated use. Improper attention was also paid to beneficial insects and other beneficial organisms.

Newer practices have attempted to minimize the harmful effects of these earlier practices. The emphasis shifted from elimination of particular pests to the suppression of pests to an economically optimum level.

Proper orchard maintenance (such as removal of debris), encouraging beneficial organisms, and accurate record keeping are essential supplements to the application of chemical agents. Perhaps most important is to understand habits and life cycles of the pests that cause damage. Likewise, it is essential to know and understand the organisms that prey on these pests.

Know Your Enemy – I'm not sure which famous general came up with the statement, "Know your enemy," but probably all generals have held this rule high on their list of important warfare rules. The same statement holds true for managing pests that inflict damage to pecan trees and pecan crops. The better understanding that you have of these pests, the better you can apply effective control methods. This doesn't mean that you need to get a Ph.D. in entomology — a few basics on insect development, life cycles, and feeding habits will help considerably. It also helps to know what the enemy looks like in its many stages from egg to larva to pupa to adult. The insect is typically a master at disguise. It also helps to know the looks of your allies as well. Few insects look as threatening as our friend the assassin bug, and few are as helpful.

Monitoring Procedures - A proper monitoring procedure for each predator is the first step in proper integrated pest management. The most common forms of insect monitoring are systematic orchard observation and the use of traps. While you are in the orchard, keep your eyes open. By understanding your enemy, you'll know better where and when to look.

Observation can be supplemented with traps. These traps are typically used for detection of the insect pests, rather than as a control feature. I guess you can say, however, that every pest trapped is one less to inflict damage.

Again, keep proper records of when, where, and how many. Soon, you'll learn when control measures are necessary. Your chemical supplier will often have published guidelines on anticipated occurrence dates and control measures. As always, your County Extension Agent will often have information on applying insecticides based on modeling and other predictive methods developed by universities and experiment facilities.

Specific monitoring procedures for specific pests listed in this publication are described within the following sections on each particular pest.

Pheromone Traps - Pheromones are chemical substances that attract the male (in most cases) population of various species. Male bugs evidently think that the most attractive female members of the race are in the area and flock in for a visit. Traps are typically shelters that have a sticky substance that entangles the unsuspecting insects that are attracted to the sensual properties of the pheromone. Hickory shuckworms and more recently, casebearers are monitored in this way.

Pests vs. Tree Anatomy - Specific pests attack different facets of the tree's anatomy. Specifically there are pests that attack the nuts; others that attack the foliage; and others that attack the woody portions of the tree. Pictures of various pests are illustrated in Volume II.

Beneficial Organisms - Preservation of beneficial organisms is critical in orchard and home pecan management. Lady beetles, lacewings, assassin bugs, spiders and other predacious organisms prey on aphids, caterpillars, and other enemies of the yard and orchard.

Birds and Mammals - Of course all of you are familiar with squirrels and their fondness for nuts. Crows and bluejays also cart off their share of the orchard proceeds. Mice and rats are also fond of pecans, and can stash up to a hundred pounds or more of our best production. All these rodents and birds are experts at judging pecan flesh. Deer and beavers attack the trees. It's no small wonder that any pecan trees are still standing.

Pictures of the pests that inflict damage to pecan are included on pages 107-126. Due the importance of these pests, I have included updated information on pecan weevil, hickory shuckworm, and pecan nut casebearer in the new text of Volume II. **A good information resource for most other insects that inflict damage to pecan is listed in the reference section of Volume II.**

Pecan Diseases

Diseases have the following effects: foliage and nut damage; reduced growth and deformation of nuts and foliage; decreased nut quality. Severe infestation can cause defoliation, shuck adherence (stick-tights) and nut abortion. Detection: olive brown to black spots/lesions form on leaves and nut shucks. In severe cases, the entire nut shuck can turn black. Leaves and shoots that show in excess of 50% surface coverage usually die.

Scab

Scab is the nemesis in growing pecans in humid areas such as the southeastern area of the United States. Scab affects both nuts and foliage.

Foliage scab occurrence - Develops in warm humid conditions as early as initial leaf expansion. Susceptibility usually decreases as leaves mature.

Nut scab occurrence - Develops in warm humid conditions from nut set until pre-harvest.

Control - proper cultivar choice, improved orchard ventilation, treatments with fungicides labeled for pecans.

Due to the importance of controlling this disease, updated information is included in the new section of Volume II. Pictures that relate to scab are also shown. Procedures for controlling scab are effective for most other pecan diseases.

Chapter 10
NUTRITION AND WATER REQUIREMENTS

Most pecan trees need supplemental nutrients to reach their potential in producing optimum yields of quality pecans. One of the most common problems facing the grower is diagnosing what nutrients are needed and in what quantity. Visual diagnosis of various nutritional deficiencies is often difficult because symptoms relating to the different nutrients are similar. Leaf analysis is currently the best means of making this diagnosis. Consult your County Agricultural Extension Agent to determine how to collect leaf samples and to get this analysis done in your locality. Specific procedures for collecting and preparing leaf samples vary slightly, depending on who provides the analysis. A part of this chapter describes general requirements for sample collection and other information relevant to leaf sample analysis.

Eliminate the Competition

Reality started in January of 1980. We had just purchased our acreage that was in part fulfillment of my pecan oriented dreams. A light dusting of snow covered the ground — just enough snow to read the activities of various forms of wildlife. I had been a naturalist of sorts for most of my life. As a youngster I had learned to recognize most of the common birds by sight, and quite a few by the tracks they left. Cottontail rabbit tracks were also easy to spot. After moving to Oklahoma from the Texas Panhandle, squirrel tracks were added to my list of recognizable footprints. Sure enough, squirrels were relatively abundant on my twenty acres. They probably knew better than I did where the pecan trees were.

This was my first pecan scouting expedition on the newly acquired property. I had read up on propagation techniques, and located a few sources of graftwood. The task now at hand was to identify pecan trees that could be propagated to improved varieties come next spring. I also looked for large native trees that might have a few nuts left behind. I was interested in what Mother Nature had dealt in the way of seedling pecans.

The squirrels must have already carted off any native production that had food value, for all I found were a very few intact pecans with weevil holes and other problems that made the insides inedible. Some tooth marks also adorned some of the empty nuts. It doesn't take a squirrel long to discard a bad nut. Still the size, shape, and shell thickness told me something about potential production from the various trees.

What I noticed most was all the work ahead of me. The land had lain untouched for a number of years. Even in winter, small trees, big trees, dead trees, brush, and weed remnants obscured most of the pecan trees. In the earlier months before frost discarded leaves from the many plants, I learned what a jungle really looked like. The most troublesome plants were the many many vines, including the poison ivy variety.

Looking back at Oklahoma pecan production history, 1980 was a relatively poor year for pecans. Even if it had been a bumper crop, I probably couldn't have harvested any due to all the brush and other obstacles.

Well, I've written almost a page of words and still nothing said about nutrition. Maybe I'm like a lawyer building a case. Well here goes. My land was blessed with Verdigris soil, some of the richest in Oklahoma. About a dozen big native pecans (30-48 inches in diameter) along pecan creek were proof of good growing conditions, at least sometime in the past. Maybe one or two of the previous land owners had given these matriarch pecans some care and attention from time to time.

Weeds, brush, vines, other tree varieties, and other stuff also liked the rich Verdigris soil. Using my binoculars to estimate shoot growth, I peered up into the canopies of the matriarch trees. Due to competing growth, the first lateral branch on many of the pecan trees was about 20 feet from ground level. The short stubby growth indicated that the pecan trees were fighting hard to get their share of the available nutrients in the soil.

Buying land had stripped away most of my cash reserves, so clearing the land was done on weekends with help from a chainsaw and an old Ford 9N tractor. I started by removing all non-pecan trees from around my best native pecans. Stump killer was used judiciously to minimize sprouting. Brush and vines were also cleared away. By 1981, I could at least see my pecan trees from a distance of more than ten feet. I had neither the time nor the funds to apply fertilizer even if I knew what to apply.

Harvest time in 1981 found me with at least enough native pecans to know what they looked like. Luckily, the pecans were at least average in size, and relatively thin shelled. Of course all of the trees produced slightly different looking nuts with different characteristics.

As the clearing progressed along with my know-how, so did the appearance of the trees and the quality of the nuts. Even during bad years, there were some nuts on the trees. 1984 was a very good year. I still didn't have any production from my grafted trees yet, but the native crop did very well. Some of the medium sized trees even set a pretty good crop. All in all, I harvested nuts from about 40 trees. Nut quality was proportional to the number of years each tree had been under management.

Eliminating the competition for nutrients from other plant life probably did more good for my pecans than the later applications of fertilizer. If I had applied fertilizer early on, little would have been absorbed by the pecan trees. I recently planted clover under the dozen or so matriarch natives to help provide additional nitrogen. These large pecan trees are difficult to manage due to their size. A smart grower would probably convert them to firewood, but I feel that they are part of the land's heritage. They also provide pollen for the improved varieties, and some good tasting nuts on a slightly irregular basis. My improved variety pecans now receive top priority.

In Oklahoma, it seems that water comes two different ways: too much and not enough. Average rainfall in our part of Oklahoma is about 35 inches per year. In my years of growing pecans here, I've seen 17 inches of rain fall in a two week period during May. Thirty inches fell in a one month period in the fall and washed much of the pecan crop away. Unlike some pecan orchards, there is enough slope on my property that water drains off rather quickly, minimizing tree damage due to long term standing water. On the other hand, I've witnessed three or four month periods without a drop. Luckily I have well water that can supplement the dry periods.

The animal kingdom can also upset the pecan grower's apple cart —or maybe it's his pecan cart. I'm talking about our industrious dam builder, the beaver. Oklahoma is the new found sanctuary of the beaver. A colony of beavers set up shop just above my fence line on Pecan Creek. I think they were pushing to get the creek renamed Beaver Creek. Between myself and a federal trapper, we had managed to stop their invasion of my property.

Pecan trees on my side of the fence line started looking sick. I couldn't figure out what was wrong until I started to dig a post hole and hit water a foot below the surface. The pesky beavers had raised the water table for a substantial distance downstream from their lake building project. Luckily one of Oklahoma's big rain storms washed their dam away, and the beavers moved further upstream. The pecan trees took several years to reestablish critical parts of their root systems.

Thus water management has some unique challenges and pecan nutrition is more than a fertilizer program. It helps to have good soil to start with, and eliminating extraneous growth is a big help. Be sure first of all that nutrients that you add to the soil and foliage find their way to the pecan trees. It's embarrassing to win first prize for growing grand champion ragweed.

Like people, pecans need proper nutrition to live a healthy life, and to produce at their best. Although some pecan cultivars are more tolerant to various nutritional deficiencies than others, all productive pecan trees will need nutritive supplements. Pecan nuts, which contain a host of nutrients, are removed from the orchard and consumed by beings other than the tree that produced them. Many naturally occurring nutrients are used up faster than they are replenished. A proper and well timed fertilization program helps to keep these nutritional needs in balance. **Placement and timing of fertilizer applications are as important as proper fertilizer selection and rate.**

Nutrition Basics

Too Much or Not Enough?

Too much fertilizer of one type can help trigger a nutritional deficiency of another type. Thus, it's important to conduct proper diagnostic procedures to determine which nutrients need to be added, and how much of each.

Diagnosing Nutritional Problems

Some experts can look at a pecan tree and probably calibrate the proper fertilizer rates to apply. I can usually tell that the tree needs **something**, but not often what or how much. Some nutrition problems are relatively easy to diagnose. Severe zinc deficiency is obvious by visual examination. However, a moderate zinc deficiency can reduce production and nut quality and be difficult to detect visually.

Symptoms for several different nutrient deficiencies look similar. It's hard to tell for sure which element is in short supply. Most pecan producing states have organizations that analyze leaf and soil samples. These tests provide accurate readings on nutrient concentrations in the pecan leaves and soils, respectively.

Leaf analysis is by far the best way to determine pecan nutritional needs in existing trees. Soil tests are best conducted before trees are planted. Any severe deficiencies in the soil can thus be treated ahead of time. Soil tests usually provide the pH as a part of the analysis. Soil pH is very important, and more will be said about it later. Soil tests conducted after the trees are in place are of little help in determining nutritional needs. Nutrient concentrations in the soil can be quite different from those absorbed by the tree.

Procedures for collecting and preparing leaf samples for analysis are included later in this chapter.

Soil pH

Soil pH indicates whether the soil is acidic or alkaline, and to what degree. A pH reading of 7.0 indicates neutral soil. In other words it is neither acidic nor alkaline. Soils in the southeastern USA are typically slightly acidic; those in the western USA are typically alkaline. Pecans do best if planted in soils that range in pH from 6.5 to 7.0. Soil pH has a significant bearing on fertilizer application and results.

Soil pH can be altered either accidentally or on purpose. Lime is usually added to acidic soils to increase pH. Sulfur lowers it. Fertilizer selection also has an effect on the pH of soils. For example, ammonium nitrate is reported to raise soil pH for a while after application; ammonium sulfate on the other hand lowers soil pH.

Chlorosis

Chlorosis is symptomatic for many of the nutritional deficiencies that are managed by the pecan grower. Chlorosis is defined as a yellowing or bleached appearance of leaf tissue due to limited chlorophyll development. Interveinal chlorosis shows chlorotic effects between major veins. Different nutritional deficiencies will cause variations in the chlorotic colors and patterns. Some chlorosis starts in older leaves while other nutrient deficiencies trigger this abnormal condition initially in new growth. The position where initial chlorosis starts can be used as a diagnostic feature.

Leaf Analysis Results

Leaf analysis provides the concentration of most of the important nutritional elements found in pecan trees. Major nutrients, including nitrogen, potassium, phosphorus, magnesium, and sulfur

are listed in percent. Micronutrients, including zinc, iron, manganese, and boron are usually listed in parts per million. Fertilizer recommendations also accompany most leaf analysis.

Nutrients Important to Pecans

Nitrogen (N)

Nitrogen is the most common element to come up short in a pecan leaf analysis. Pecan trees use substantial nitrogen for both growth and nut production. Nitrogen deficient trees usually have lighter colored foliage than trees with adequate nitrogen. Severe deficiency can cause leaves to turn yellow or pinkish in color. A shortage of nitrogen also reduces shoot growth, reduces flowering, and decreases nut size and quality.

What is enough nitrogen? The answer varies with climactic conditions and other factors. Specialists in each pecan producing state have preferred ranges of nitrogen concentration. The range, as determined from a leaf analysis, varies from 2.3% dry weight to 4.0%. A value of 2.8% falls within everybody's range. A common recommendation for mature trees that are under a fertilization program is about 100 to 150 pounds of actual nitrogen per acre per year.

Too much nitrogen can also cause problems. Added shoot growth from nitrogen applications can induce deficiencies in other elements such as phosphorus and potassium. These deficiencies result from a dilution of the other elements within the more rapidly growing shoot. Nitrogen leaf scorch is another problem that has shown up in some areas of the southeastern USA. If recommendations from a leaf analysis are used to gauge the amount of supplemental nitrogen, problems from excess nitrogen are rare.

Anhydrous ammonia (rarely used in orchards) and various granular fertilizers such as ammonium sulfate are sources of nitrogen that can be applied in an orchard environment. Fertilizers are commonly packaged as mixtures of nitrogen, phosphorus, and potassium. Based on other nutritional needs, granular supplements such as 26-4-8 are cost effective. Percent nitrogen is the first of the three numbers (26% in this case).

Planting legumes such as clover and vetch will also add nitrogen to the soil. This practice is becoming more common because of increases in chemical fertilizer cost and environmental issues. Legumes also play a dual role in encouraging beneficial organisms.

Potassium (K)

Essential in both tree growth and nut production, adequate potassium is a must. In areas with significant rainfall and humidity, much of the available potassium has been leached from the soil. These conditions occur most frequently in the southeastern USA. Soils in the midwestern and southwestern USA are usually higher in available potassium. Recommended leaf concentrations of potassium range from .75% to about 1.5%.

Potassium deficiency sometimes occurs when nitrogen fertilizer is applied without sufficient potassium. Deficiency shows up initially as irregular interveinal chlorosis. Older leaves are the first to show symptoms. Chlorosis may move later into younger leaves. Potassium deficiency in the foliage may become more severe during nut filling because potassium is transported to the nuts rather than to the leaves and shoots. Nut shucks have up to 86 percent of the tree's available potassium. Severe potassium deficiency may result in pronounced leaf scorch, premature defoliation, and shoot dieback. Reduced nut quality and size may also result from insufficient potassium.

Potassium can be added to the soil in the form of KCl (potassium chloride), potassium oxide, or other potassium/potash compounds. In mixed granular fertilizers, potassium concentration is the third number; for example, 26-4-8 contains 8 percent potassium oxide (6.6% K). Several years may lapse between the application of potassium and its assimilation into the soil and finally into the trees. This assimilation occurs more rapidly in sandy soils than in clay soils. Foliar applications of potassium are reported to be ineffective.

Excess potassium may result in an imbalance of magnesium, calcium, and other elements.

Phosphorus (P)

Phosphorus deficiency is rare in pecans. Geographically, deficiencies are more common in humid regions of the Southeast than in the central and western USA. Phosphorus is more likely to be deficient in light textured soils. Soils fertilized with mixtures, for example 13-13-13, will retain more phosphorus than nitrogen or potassium. Losses of phosphorus due to natural depletion and crop assimilation are small compared with many other nutrients.

Phosphorus is required for the production of both wood tissues and nuts. Concentrations of phosphorus in leaf tissue may be one third the amount found in nuts. Leaf concentrations of phosphorus (as determined from a leaf analysis) should be generally greater than .12 percent. Again, each state has its own recommendations. Most states recommend a minimum value of .12% to a maximum value of .18%. Texas (mid 1990s) had an upper limit recommendation of .3%.

Increased phosphorus deficiency in leaves and shoots may show up during kernel filling, especially with heavy crops. Severe phosphorus deficiency causes yellow to pale green color in young spring foliage. Leaves that have a bluish to purplish tint are also symptomatic of deficient phosphorus. Low phosphorus is also reported to be a major cause of leaf scorch, defoliation, and increased susceptibility to cold injury.

Too much phosphorus can inhibit the assimilation of copper and the uptake of nitrogen. Excess phosphorus has been reported to contribute to zinc deficiency. High phosphorus levels may convert available zinc to insoluble zinc phosphate. This reaction can occur both in the soil and in the tree. I observed this situation in my orchard before reducing the phosphorus levels in my fertilizer program. Foliar sprays with zinc compounds corrected the problem.

Phosphorus deficiencies are best handled before pecan trees are planted. If required, phosphorus supplements can be applied to the soil in the form of super-phosphates or other forms of phosphorus (P_2O_5). In mixed granular fertilizers, phosphorus is the middle number. For example, 26-4-8 contains 4 percent P_2O_5. Phosphorus additives are assimilated slowly into the soil, and will typically last for several years. Since downward movement of phosphorus into the soil is slow, it is best applied as deeply into the soil as possible. Monoammonium phosphate (MAP) is a soluble form of phosphorus that can be applied to the soil or used as a foliar spray. The effectiveness of foliar applied phosphorous is questionable.

Subsequent surface applications may likewise be in place for several years before their effect is reflected in a leaf analysis.

Zinc

Conversations among pecan enthusiasts will inevitably turn to zinc at one time or another. Zinc may be rated as the mystery element of pecan culture. Concentrations of zinc, like other Micronutrients required by pecans, are usually referenced in micrograms per gram or in parts per million (ppm) — which amount to the same thing. A microgram is a millionth of a gram – or a thousandth of a milligram.

Required zinc levels for pecans exceed that of many other plant forms. It is a component required for several different pecan systems, including flowering, nut development, leaf growth, and shoot growth. Recommended leaf analysis readings generally range from a minimum of 50 ppm to a maximum of 150 ppm. Some western states list higher minimum and maximum levels. Zinc deficiency is more difficult to treat in western environments where soils have a high pH.

Severe zinc deficiencies are relatively easy to diagnose, but even slight deficiencies can reduce tree performance. Slight deficiencies may go unnoticed by even the most astute grower – all the more reason to do regular leaf analysis.

Severe zinc deficiency is characterized by chlorosis and curling of young leaves, along with shoot dieback in some cases. Some forms of zinc deficiency are referenced as pecan rosette. Wavy leaf margins are also characteristic of zinc deficiency, as illustrated in *Figure N-4*. Other pictures of zinc deficiency are illustrated in *Figures N-3 and N-6*. These illustrations can be found on page 103.

These examples of zinc deficiency were purposely induced by high applications of phosphorus.

Soil applications of zinc compounds are effective in regions of the southeastern USA, and other areas where soil pH is below 7.0. Western areas that have high soil pH require foliar applications of supplemental zinc. Zinc sulfate (36%) is commonly used for both ground and foliar application. Zinc nitrate, zinc chelate, and commercial nitrogen-zinc combinations are also used.

Soil applications of between 5 and ten pounds of zinc sulfate per mature tree are typical in lower pH soils. Zinc chelate is reported in some sources to be superior in higher pH soils, since this formulation of zinc is released more slowly than with zinc sulfate. Less zinc thus gets tied up in the soil as insoluble compounds. Tree response to a zinc soil treatment may take two or more years.

Foliar application is the common practice for western and central USA pecan producing areas. Rates of application for zinc sulfate are about six pounds per acre. For dilute applications, mix one pound of zinc sulfate to fifty gallons of water. Pre-mix the zinc sulfate in a five gallon pail with three or so gallons of water before putting it into the sprayer tank. Adding one pint of a liquid nitrogen solution per 50 gallons of spray will provide better foliar zinc absorption. Commercial nitrogen-zinc compounds are also available for foliar use. These compounds should be applied according to instructions on the label.

Good foliar coverage is essential since zinc does not migrate within the tree. Three to six foliar treatments per year may be needed to meet zinc requirements. Spray programs should start soon after budbreak, and continue at regular intervals (two to three weeks apart) until shoot and leaf expansion slows or stops. The under sides of leaves absorb more zinc, so sprays are best directed from the ground upwards. As with all sprays, treatment during pollination is discouraged. Timing and frequency of zinc application depends on tree age, degree of deficiency, and other local factors. Consult your County Agricultural Extension Agent for recommendations.

In some areas, such as northern Oklahoma, once a month appears to be adequate. Mid to late July here in northern Oklahoma is the point when I stop my zinc spray program, I personally wait until about the first of May for the first application. Leaves are big enough by then to catch a substantial part of the spray.

Calcium (Ca)

Calcium as a nutrient is usually present in sufficient amounts. Lime, a compound of calcium, is commonly applied to increase the pH of soils. Recommended levels of calcium in a leaf analysis range from .7% to 1.5%, and sometimes higher, for some of the western states and Louisiana.

Calcium sulfate can be added to the soil as a nutrient supplement without increasing the pH.

Magnesium (Mg)

Magnesium is sometimes found to be deficient in acidic soils, such as those of the southeastern USA. Soils fertilized heavily with lime and potassium may be especially vulnerable to magnesium deficiency. See the section below on the potassium-calcium-magnesium triad. Acceptable magnesium levels from a leaf analysis should range from .3 – .6 percent. Soils of the southwestern and midwestern USA normally have a higher pH and are not usually deficient in magnesium.

Symptoms of magnesium deficiency include a pronounced interveinal chlorosis contrasting with darker green veinal areas. Christmas tree patterns are formed on affected leaves.

Dolomitic limestone is recommended as a preplanting soil additive to prevent magnesium deficiency. Another form of supplement is magnesium sulfate (Epsom salt). It is more water soluble than dolomitic limestone. Foliar sprays containing magnesium have also been used, but are reported to be less effective than soil treatment. Since assimilation of magnesium by pecan trees can be a slow process, correction of magnesium deficiency may take several years.

Sulfur

Pecan trees utilize sulfur for growth and nut development. Deficiency of sulfur in pecan trees is rare. Sulfur is a component in many fertilizer formulations, and is thus added to the soil and foliage along with target elements. Atmospheric pollution also adds its share of sulfur to the environment. Recommended concentrations in a pecan leaf analysis range from .1 to .25 percent. Some reports indicate that sulfur concentrations below .2% in leaves correlate with a decline in tree growth. Agricultural forms of elemental sulfur can be used to lower soil pH.

Iron

Pecans, like other plant life, require iron for photosynthesis. Chlorophyll, the green substance in leaves, has iron in its composition. Chlorophyll is essential in the production of carbohydrates through photosynthesis. Carbohydrates are in turn essential for tree health and nut production.

Iron levels in a leaf analysis should be greater than 50 ppm. Iron shortages are most common in cool, wet weather — usually in the spring. These shortages may disappear as the season progresses and weather gets warmer. High concentrations of zinc, manganese, and phosphorus may contribute to iron deficiency in pecans. High pH soils are also more prone to be associated with iron deficiency.

Symptoms of iron deficiency include chlorosis of leaf tissue. Color may vary from pale green to yellow. Veins in affected leaves may be an intense shade of green, although this is not always the case. Young leaves are the first to show symptoms of iron deficiency.

Since iron is common in most soils, treatment for iron deficiency is directed at correcting conditions that inhibit iron uptake – such as lowering the soil pH, and adjusting fertilizer rates and composition. Foliar applications of iron chelate and other recommended iron compounds are also effective.

Other Micronutrients

Although copper, manganese, and boron are necessary nutrients for pecan growth and tree health, deficiencies of these elements are rarely a problem. Excess boron in soils and irrigation water sometimes occurs in western pecan regions. Too much boron can affect tree health, including marginal leaf scorch, shoot dieback, and premature defoliation. Molybdenum and chlorine are also required Micronutrients. A deficiency of nickel has been reported to cause mouse-ear, a disease which results in abnormal plant growth. Leaflets on the rachis resemble mouse ears. See page 2 for additional detail and illustrations.

General Fertilization Guidelines (Flying Blind)

– Or maybe I should say fertilizing blind. All too often pecans and other plants are fertilized without the benefit of a leaf analysis. For cases where leaf analysis is not available or not practical, some general guidelines for nutrient supplements are needed.

In average soils, pecan trees may be fertilized at a rate of one pound of granular mixed fertilizer per inch of trunk diameter. Trees above 15 inches in diameter may require up to two pounds of fertilizer per inch of trunk diameter. Older trees that produce heavily may even require up to three pounds per inch of trunk diameter. Fertilizers specially formulated for pecans are available from different suppliers. Some of these mixes contain the Micronutrients mentioned above. You can also mix your own from various common formulations.

Zinc deficiency is a common problem for the pecan grower. In soils with pH readings below 7.0, 36% zinc sulfate or zinc chelate can be applied to the soil at a rate of a half pound per inch of trunk diameter. Foliar sprays of 36% zinc sulfate or commercial zinc products may also be applied, especially if pH levels exceed 7.0. Applications of zinc chelate to higher pH soils can also help to control pecan zinc deficiency. **Follow instructions on the label.**

Applying Fertilizers

Preliminary Soil Preparation

As discussed earlier, a soil test should be conducted before pecan trees are planted. This is especially true if an orchard or several trees are to be planted. Even in a yard environment, a soil test is not a bad investment. It can help in vegetable gardening, flower beds, and other horticultural activities besides growing pecans.

Soil pH can be determined and if practical, adjusted accordingly. All deficient nutrients with the exception of nitrogen should be adjusted to recommended levels. Examples include phosphorus and potassium. Other potential problems may surface from a soil analysis. In some cases, the soil just may not be suitable for pecans. It's better to know this fact up front than to spend money on a project that is sure to fail.

Fertilizer Placement

Where do I put my fertilizer? —Granular fertilizers are best applied over an area under the tree that reaches one to three feet on both sides of the tree drip line, depending on tree size. The drip line is at the tips of the outermost tree branches. If branches were like a rain-proof roof, the drip line is where the rain would drip to the ground. Fertilizers can be worked into the top four to six inches of the soil, or most types can be applied to the surface. Irrigation or rain will carry the fertilizer to the feeder roots. Feeder roots are most prevalent six to eighteen inches below the surface. After seven or eight years in an orchard environment, fertilizer can be applied to the entire orchard floor.

Urea can be used as a surface application if temperatures are below 80° F and soil pH is below 7.0. Anhydrous ammonia should not be applied to the soil surface since most of it will be lost as gaseous ammonia.

Timing

When should I apply my fertilizer? – Fertilizers are usually applied in late winter from mid January through mid March. This helps to ensure the availability of supplemental nutrients before growth starts in the spring. Timing is somewhat dependent on fertilizer type, and when spring comes to your area. Some nitrogen fertilizers are assimilated quickly, and should be applied just before budbreak. Fertilizer for young trees may be split into two applications, one in late winter and one in late May to early June. Fertilizer applied late in the year may delay dormancy, and thus subject trees to increased freeze damage susceptibility. Recommendations for fertilizing in the fall vary from state to state, so consult your local specialist.

Fertilizer Formulations

Packaged fertilizers come in various mixes, such as 13-13-13, 10-20-10, 10-10-10, 34-0-0, etc. Most Farmers Co-op Organizations and other fertilizer suppliers can mix common nutrients such as nitrogen, potassium, and phosphorus to your specifications, provided that the desired quantity is large enough.

Record keeping

Preaching about keeping records is about as popular as telling your children that they can't eat pizza anymore. Still, the grower who keeps accurate records will usually be more successful than one who doesn't. Records were mentioned back in pest management. This doesn't mean that if you keep pest management records you're exempt from keeping nutrition records. Soil tests, leaf analysis, fertilizer types, rates, and dates are all important records to keep. Production records and shoot growth records are also important. Records can tell if you're doing things right or if you need to seek out other information and try something different. I said different because we pecan growers never do anything wrong.

Other General Comments

Fertilization rates and recommended types vary significantly across the country. Your County Agricultural Extension Agent should have suggestions for growing conditions that apply in your area.

Proper fertilization is reflected in tree appearance, production, and other observable factors. Tree foliage should have a healthy green appear-ance; nuts should be well developed and have plump straw colored kernels (depending on cultivar). Properly fertilized pecans exhibit better shucksplit than undernourished pecans.

Fertilizers can't create magic. They can't overcome serious water deficiency, and they can't turn eighteen inches of soil into ten feet of proper growing media. Nor can they overcome serious overcrowding and lack of sunlight. Establishing and maintaining proper nutrition is, however, part of good pecan management. It applies whether you have one tree or ten thousand.

Collecting Soil Samples

Soil analysis is often done only before an orchard is established or before trees in general are planted. If trees aren't responding to fertilization recommended by leaf analysis, additional soil tests may be helpful. State and County Extension Offices usually have procedures for collecting and submitting soil samples. They also have information sheets to complete, and some have containers for the sample.

Collecting Leaf Samples

Leaf analysis, (also called tissue analysis) provides the best recommendations for fertilization. Your County Agricultural Agent should be able to tell you how to collect the sample(s), and how to get them analyzed. An interpretation of the result is usually provided which tells the element concentrations, and the amount of fertilizer required to correct any deficiencies.

It is best not to mix leaves from different cultivars together. Collect samples that are representative of the area being analyzed.

Pecan Water Requirements

Pecans grow without irrigation along creek and river bottoms in areas that receive only thirty inches or so of annual rainfall. In the western parts of the USA and the more arid foreign locations, irrigation is a must. Drought stress can occur even in areas with substantial rainfall. In the southeastern USA where rainfall reaches fifty inches per year— and more, pecans will produce higher yields of better quality nuts if supplemental water is provided during dry periods. Too much water and changes in the water table, either up or down, can also affect pecan tree health and nut production. **Thus the right amount of water is certainly a critical factor in pecan management. Remember also that underground water is a valuable resource. Use it wisely.**

Water Utilization

Like all plants – and animals, pecan trees require water for basic survival. Too little water or too much water can cause significant stress, and continued stress can cause pecan trees to die. Most pecan feeder roots that absorb water usually lie within the top 24 inches of soil. Water management in this soil zone is especially critical to pecan production and tree health. If the soil becomes too dry or too wet in this zone, feeder roots become less efficient. Prolonged drought or "wet feet" may cause feeder roots to die, and adversely affects other components of the root system.

Feeder roots frequently die off in one area and expand in other areas as water conditions change in the tree's microenvironment. If water conditions change rapidly, tree metabolism and growth will be affected while new feeder roots are being regenerated. If drought or excess moisture extend over a long time period, then tree systems above the ground will be similarly affected. Portions of the canopy will die back and both the current crop and future production will be adversely affected. Water is required for uptake of nutrients from the soil. Too much or too little water can inhibit this uptake, causing nutrient deficiencies of various kinds. Water is also required for basic plant functions, such as photosynthesis, cooling the plant surfaces, and for growth. **What is enough water? What is too much water? Those are good questions, but the answers are often difficult.**

Effects of Drought on Nut Production

Drought stress can affect nuts in two basic ways, depending on when the stress occurs. Too little water during the early growth period (nut sizing) can cause nuts to be small. Too little water during the late growth period can cause nuts to be poor-

ly filled. Insufficient water in the latest stages of nut development can inhibit or interfere with shuck split.

Factors Affecting Water Availability

Many factors determine how much water is needed to successfully grow pecan trees and produce good quality nuts. Some obvious ones are:

1. Humidity levels – High humidity results in less loss of water by evaporation and transpiration.

2. Transpiration rate – Transpiration relates to water that is given off through leaves and other plant surfaces. As the soil surface dries, most water loss is through transpiration.

3. Wind velocities – Water loss increases as wind velocity increases.

4. Temperature – Water loss increases with increased temperature.

Soil Moisture

Virtually all moisture for trees is supplied via the root system. Roots absorb moisture that is held in the soil. Different soils hold different amounts of water. Sandy soils hold less water than clay or clay loam soils. Soils that are rich in organic matter have good moisture retention. The amount of water used by pecan trees is essentially limited to what can be absorbed from the soil. During peak usage periods such as nut filling, a mature tree can utilize more than 300 gallons per day. If demand exceeds supply, drought stress sets in.

Different soils retain different amounts of water. County Soil Survey books publish important properties for soils in the USA. Water holding capacity and average percolation rates (a function of soil permeability) are among the most important factors where water is concerned. After soils are saturated, then runoff occurs. Rainfall that doesn't soak into the soil is basically lost as far as pecan trees are concerned. Thus trees can utilize only part of the moisture from rains that come several inches at a time. During May of 1993, our part of Oklahoma received over 17 inches of rain. Of the 17 inches, probably 6 or 7 inches at the most were actually utilized by pecan trees. Of course the rest filled all the ponds and reservoirs in the area. The stored water was used in July and August when we had no rain at all. Fortunately, a gentle slope on my property helps to provide adequate drainage. Soils remain water saturated for only a few hours after a heavy rain.

Water Percolation, Retention, and Drainage

Water percolates through the soil at different rates and to different depths, again depending on soil composition. Water percolates faster in coarse textured soils than in fine textured soils. Fine textured soils hold more water and supply more moisture to trees. A two inch rain might permeate clay loam soil for a depth of two feet, provided that it came down slow enough to avoid runoff.

The utilization of moisture applied by Mother Nature in the form of rain, snow, and ice is dependent on the local soil composition, internal drainage, and surface slope. It also depends on the rate that the moisture reaches the soil surface. Thus a key factor in water management is to maintain soils close to their water holding capacity, and yet avoid soil saturation, at least for extended periods. In areas that are subject to flooding or excessive rainfall, steps must be taken to provide adequate internal and surface drainage.

Problems From Excess Water

Rainfall is in some ways like the forward pass in football. Two out of the three possible results can be harmful to the final outcome. Rain in the right amount is like a completed pass; it's hard to beat. If all rains contribute to filling the water holding capacity of the soil, then rainfall is extremely helpful. If they contribute to maintaining soil saturation, rains can contribute to the demise of the grower. Too much water is often more difficult to deal with than not enough water.

Water saturation displaces essential oxygen from the soil. Oxygen is essential for basic tree metabolism. Without oxygen, absorption of moisture

and nutrients cease, causing a condition much like severe drought stress. Without aeration, carbon dioxide also builds up in the soil, contributing to the deterioration of larger roots. As roots die, essential hormones that stimulate root and shoot growth are not produced, causing upward growth to cease. Poor soil aeration contributes to buildup of toxins and salts to a damaging level.

These problems can be observed in flooded areas. A pond that I constructed filled in August. It covered almost the entire root area of one pecan tree, and half of the root area of another. The tree that has most of its roots covered showed signs of stress within a few weeks. Almost total leaf drop occurred during early October, ahead of other nearby trees. The tree failed to leaf out in the spring, and was totally dead within the year.

The other tree suffered all of the symptoms mentioned above in gradual stages. Branches and leaves on the water saturated side of the tree stopped growth within a few weeks. Early leaf drop on the water covered side was prevalent. The next year, the water saturated side of the tree had severe dieback. The tree as a whole grew very slowly for several years and failed to produce nuts. Now the tree is regaining its health. New branches are gradually replacing those that had succumbed as a result of saturated soil. Evidently, new roots were developing outside the water saturated area.

Irrigation

The rate and position of supplemental water supplied by man can be controlled, at least until tree demand exceeds system capacity. Water supplied by man is termed irrigation. Irrigation water can be less beneficial than rainfall since it sometimes carries contaminant that may be harmful to pecans.

Irrigation Basics

Irrigation can be simple or complex, depending on the amount of water that needs to be supplied, the area to be covered, and many other factors. This chapter covers some of the common forms of irrigation. It is not within the scope of this book to describe how to design and construct irrigation systems. Such guides are available from many of the State Agricultural Extension Organizations. The Texas Agricultural Extension Service offers an excellent brochure.

Irrigation scheduling is usually based on soil moisture or on evaporation rates. If available moisture drops below about half of the soil holding capacity, tree stress starts to occur. In normal circumstances, soil moisture increases slightly with depth. The top two feet of soil in eastern and central parts of pecan country hold an average of about 2.7 inches of available moisture. Western soils typically hold less moisture. Daily rates of application vary from less than a tenth of an inch in winter up to almost a half inch where summers are hot and dry.

The goal of any irrigation system is to deliver a specified amount of water to the target plants within a specified amount of time. There are several ways to accomplish this objective.

Kinds of Irrigation

A few trees in the yard – Irrigation can be as simple as running sprinklers until a can under the sprinklers has caught a designated amount of water. Once delivery time is determined, water can usually be applied correctly without the can. A homeowner can also get a soaker hose and apply water for a specified time. It's not too hard to figure out how much water comes through a soaker hose in a designated time period. Stick the soaker hose in a trash can, turn on the water, and measure how much comes out in a minute. After a while, a homeowner can estimate soil moisture by sight and touch, and come fairly close to applying the right amount of water. Just remember to avoid saturating the soil for extended periods.

On the other hand, don't be fooled into thinking that if your pecans are deprived of water that they will send roots to China and extract it there. Excessive drought will adversely affect your trees. Unstressed trees are happy trees, and happy trees are more attractive and produce more nuts.

Flood irrigation – Basically, flood irrigation covers the surface of the orchard until a designated amount of water has been applied or until water allocated by the water district runs out. Water for flood irrigation is often applied over a short time duration, but time intervals between irrigation cycles may be long. Flood irrigation may subject trees to excess water for a time. If water is in short supply, levees are sometimes built around each tree to better focus the applied water. This is often the case in young orchards.

Sprinkler systems – Sprinkler systems for pecan orchards can resemble yard sprinkler systems — only on a larger scale. There are several designs, and you or your contractor can determine which one is best for your situation. Design is dependent on orchard size, the rate water can be supplied, terrain, and other factors. Like in yards, systems are usually partitioned so that sections of the orchard can be irrigated in sequence.

Drip or Trickle Irrigation – Drip systems apply water through low volume distribution devices called an emitter. Microsprinklers and microsprayers are also used to deliver water. Application requires longer time periods than with sprinklers to deliver equal water volumes. These smaller doses of water are intended to replace water at the same rate that it is used up. Still with a drip system, water should be turned off of a particular section for an average of twelve hours per day to minimize oxygen depletion and other problems that occur with saturated soils. Most drip systems are also laid out in sections, so the "off" time can be a function of system design.

Microsprayers and microsprinklers (micros) are also becoming more common, and deliver water at rates of up to ten gallons per hour. Like yard sprayers and sprinklers, these devices can cover variable sized areas. As trees grow in size, coverage can be expanded. Clogging is less of a problem also. Like their larger counterparts, evaporation is greater with micro-delivery than with an emitter.

44

Irrigation Strategies

Try to apply approximately half of the water holding capacity of the soil each time you irrigate. For most soils this averages 1.25 to 1.75 inches.

In many parts of pecan country, irrigation is required only during parts of the season. When the ground starts to dry out in spring, turn the system on to bring the soil to its ideal water capacity. From then through nut maturity, monitor soil moisture and apply irrigation when necessary. Try not to let the trees get stressed from either not enough or too much water. Of course sometimes demand exceeds supply. Wells can run low or run dry. Sometimes reservoirs exceed their flood pools and trees get flooded for longer periods than we like. There's not much we can do about this event either.

Often, irrigation is terminated too early in the fall, especially when weather starts to cool. This action may result in poor shucksplit. These stick-tights may be a result of early freezes, insufficient water, or both. On the other hand, late water may contribute to late dormancy and encourages freeze damage. This happens most often when trees are stressed in the summer and initiate a new spurt of growth when the weather cools and more moisture is available.

Learn to recognize when your trees are stressed. Local conditions cause subtle appearance changes that are diagnostic of too little or too much water. Trees have a way of letting you know when they need attention. Pecan culture occurs in a dynamic environment. Procedures that are good today may be inadequate in months and years to come.

Chapter 11
PECANS FOR FOOD

This is what it's all about — growing nuts for sale or personal consumption. I've included most of the pertinent information regarding food in my book: _When A Man's Fancy Turns to Cooking_, published in 1996.

I've found several good reasons for this. One relates to the fact that cooking is often messy – a good way to spill all sorts of stuff on your pretty pecan book. Another relates to the fact that a domestic quarrel might break out when the orchardist tries to take the book into the field in the middle of his/her spouse's pecan pie preparation. Why not buy the cookbook and save all these potential hazards. I'll give you a good deal!

That's All Folks – for Volume I Highlights

So there you have it— highlights from my first book on pecans, including pictures— both pretty and informative, from Volume I which follow on the next pages. Then comes the new stuff! Volume II covers updates on the Volume I technology highlights, and of course, lots of new stories, pictures, and other informative information.

Volume II Synopsis

The previous summary of my first book contains much of the information required to have a basic knowledge of the different elements of pecan culture. Volume II will attempt to augment this basic description with relevant elements of pecan culture that have been discovered/developed in the decade since my first book was published. I've also included additional cultivar color pictures, many of which are still planted in areas across the country. I have done extensive research both in my own orchard, and studying literature. While my book covers what I feel are the more relevant aspects, reference sources listed in this publication provide much additional detail and other useful information. Remember, your County Agricultural Extension Agent is still one of the best sources of advice for your particular situation.

I have attempted to provide pictures and a comprehensive description of many of the northern and ultra-northern cultivars – attempting where possible to remove some of the ambiguities in this important subset of pecan cultivars.

Volume II Contents

Chapter 1

PECAN CULTIVARS (VARIETIES)

Earlier information (page 23) provides basic information on the various categories of pecan. I have subdivided the cultivar descriptions and pictures into two basic categories — standard and northern.

Two cultivar layout/primary cultivars

Two separate formats arc provided for the pictures and "passports." Passports, like the human counterpart, provide basic information about each cultivar. The two cultivar format includes cultivars that are perhaps the best of the best, or have other special properties. These formats provide pictures of four views of the nut/kernel. A schematic describes elements of the different views. Also included are pictures of the pecan fruit (nut within the shuck) and dormant scions of one year old wood. Buds and in-shuck properties for the various cultivars are often distinctive and can help in cultivar identification.

Abbreviated format/ secondary cultivars

My book also provides an abbreviated layout of additional cultivars. These views show two views of the in-shell nut, and the dorsal (top) view of the kernel. Passport information is also provided. Most of these cultivars are fairly common across pecan country, but I personally feel that they have one or more properties that keep them from being one of the "best of the best." I've included cultivars that I feel show promise, and are worth a trial planting for further evaluation. Then there are a few that I consider in the "undesirable" category. It's helpful to know what these specimens look like also.

Properties of the Rice Farm

The author has at least one tree of almost all cultivars listed in this book. My soils are some of the best in Oklahoma, and good growth is typically experienced. It's helpful to observe properties of different cultivars at one site. The reader should note, however, that cultivar properties vary from location to location.

Characteristics of Nuts Displayed

Please note that extreme care was exercised to maintain proper scale for all nuts and kernels displayed. This makes comparisons with individual samples much easier. Nuts in the displays are mostly what I call "show nuts" — i.e. some of the better representative samples. Of course, nut quality and size vary from year to year and with climatic conditions.

Cultivar Selections

The following selections include many of the better known cultivars, and represent pecan varieties that are generally recommended for both yard plantings, and commercial production. However, after intensive natural selection and breeding, there is still no perfect cultivar. Cultivar performance is often correlated to climatic conditions. The best performing cultivars in northern climates are not ideally suited for southern climates, and vice versa. The same holds true for the more arid western climates, contrasted with humid conditions in the southeastern USA. The following pictures and descriptions are separated into the following categories:

Category 1 — Standard Cultivars

This category includes cultivars that are widely planted, and are known to many growers. Each has one or more redeeming characteristics that encourage propagation. Within this category are subclasses which are preferred for different climatic conditions. Some cultivars can be commercially successful across several regions. Cultivars suited for specific regions are so indicated on the respective color plates. When choosing cultivars to plant in a specific region, one should consider scab/disease resistance, nut maturity, etc. For example, cultivars with low scab resistance should not usually be planted in humid climates.

Category 2 — Cold Tolerant Standard Cultivars

Some standard cultivars are suitable for climatic regions with shorter growing seasons, and colder winter temperatures than what many people consider as "pecan country." These areas include parts of Oklahoma, and most of Kansas, Missouri, Kentucky, and other states within a similar latitude range. Pecan growers in higher altitudes might also wish to consider this class of cultivars.

Category 3 — Northern and Ultra-Northern Cultivars

Some cultivars are best suited only for northern climates. While these cultivars will probably grow and produce in southern climates on a regular basis, nut size, percent kernel, and other factors likely will inhibit the commercial profitability of these cultivars. Some, however, make a splendid tree for yard specimens. Ultra-northern cultivars - a term that I use to reference cultivars that can survive and produce nuts as far north as agricultural zone 4, can extend the area for pecan production considerably.

Zone Map

The zone map, located on page 51 shows the major pecan producing regions and climatic areas.

For local cultivar recommendations, the grower should consult with Agricultural Extension Agents, or other specialists. General guidelines are as follows:

Southeast — Scab resistance is recognized by many growers and researchers as an essential property for profitable pecan production. Many cultivars that have adequate scab resistance in other regions will experience severe infection in the Southeast. Foliage retention and foliage health are essential to provide optimum crop yields, nut quality, and reduce alternate bearing – thus cultivars with resistance to mites and aphids (black and yellow) are also highly desirable.

East-central, Central, and South-central — Standard cultivars are typically acceptable. Disease resistant cultivars are preferable for local areas with humid conditions or poor air circulation. Northerly portions of these areas should consider cold tolerant cultivars.

West — Cultivars that are noted for western, dry climates are preferable.

North — Northern cultivars, and some ultra-northern cultivars are preferable. Select disease resistant (scab ratings three or less) for humid areas.

Far-north — Select ultra-northern cultivars for best performance. Some northern cultivars will survive and provide crops on a less regular basis.

Intermittent Yard Plantings & Groves — This area typically represents higher altitude and/or colder climatic environments. Northern, ultra-northern, and cultivars recommended for higher elevations will typically perform best in these areas. Some commercial orchards and yard specimens will produce nuts on a regular basis when proper cultivars are selected.

Other Areas — I've personally observed or participated in pecan plantings in Nebraska, Virginia, Ohio, Utah, Colorado, Michigan, Idaho, New Jersey, and other localities thought to be far outside "pecan country." With proper cultivar selection and cultural practices, pecans can survive and produce nuts.

Cold tolerance/ early nut maturity

I must admit that the northern and ultra-northern pecan cultivars are some of the more interesting to study. These cultivars hold particular significance in pecan breeding objectives. Besides extending pecan production to colder geographic regions, early maturing cultivars provide a benefit to all areas where pecans are grown. Leaf retention is important to provide carbohydrates and other nutrients for the following year's crops. These nutrients also improve winter hardiness and tree survival under stressed conditions. Breeding for early nut maturity is one of several important objectives of the USDA Pecan Breeding and Genetics Group.

Cultivar Passports

Many of the cultivar attributes are self explanatory, including origin, nut size, percent kernel, and nut maturity (shuck split).

Shuck split variations

Since nut ripening dates have a significant relation to cultivar selection for different climatic regions, these dates are referenced to 'Stuart' for standard cultivars, and 'Colby' for northern cultivars. 'Stuart' trees are familiar to many growers, and ripening success is well documented across the country. The same holds true for 'Colby' in northern climates. These average dates are listed as days before (-) or after (+) the above reference cultivars. Again, these relative dates have been determined for the most part from my orchard in Osage County, Oklahoma, and are in general agreement with other documentation.

Scab/disease resistance

Scab susceptibility is referenced on a **scale of 1 to 5, where "1" indicates the most resistance to scab.** Other diseases, such as powdery mildew, vein spot, and brown spot, are less debilitating to pecan production. Treatment for these other diseases is often the same as for scab. Typically, cultivars with scab ratings above 2.5 – 3 should not be used in humid areas.

Scab ratings for the Southeast – Cultivars that perform well in other regions (scab ratings: 1-2) will often experience extreme infection in the Southeast. As a result, I have defined three other levels within the highest resistance category. Rating 1-S indicates superior resistance; 1-E indicates excellent resistance; 1-G represents very good resistance. At present, these ratings apply to the most resistant cultivars; however, cultivar resistance often changes with time.

Precocity

Precocity is similarly rated on a scale of 1-5, where 5 is the least precocious. Precocity indicates the time required for nut production to begin. Typically, standard cultivars come into production earlier than northern cultivars. Cultivars with ratings of "5" often take as much as ten years to produce a pound of nuts.

Nut and tree quality

These ratings are again from 1-5, where "1" indicates the better quality characteristics. Nut attributes include: cracking quality, kernel color and texture, suture strength, etc. See page 11 for further information. Tree quality includes: resistance to wind and ice damage, tree structure (willowy, upright, etc.) and other factors that relate to appearance and ease of management.

SUMMARY OF CULTIVAR ATTRIBUTES

Variety	Flow-ering	Preco-city	Scab	Nut size	% ker-nel	Nut maturity	Nut quality	Tree quality	Freeze tolerance	Origin
Lucas	II	1	1	108	49	-36	2	3	1	OH, 1965
Norton	II	4	2	76	44	-31	4	2	1	MO, 1912
Osage	I	2	1	85	54	-31	2	3	2	TX, 1989
Peruque	I	2	2	79	59	-27	2	2	1	MO, 1953
Colby	II	3	3+	62	45	-25	4	2	1	IL, 1957
Hirschi	I	2	3-	72	49	-22	3	1	1	MO, 1940
Posey	II	4	1	68	56	-18	2	1	1	IN, 1911
Pawnee	I	3	2	50	57	-17	2	2	2	TX, 1985
Major	I	4	1	79	49	-15	2	2	1	KY, 1908
Mount	II	2	2	75	52	-13	2	2	2	OK, 1966
Giles	I	2	3-	74	52	-12	3	4	1	KS, 1930
Dooley	I	2	2	79	47	-11	1	2	2	OK, 1945
Mohawk	II	2	2	44	57	-8	3	3	4	TX, 1965
Caddo	I	3	2+	70	56	-6	1+	2	2	TX, 1968
Maramec	II	3	3	48	57	-4	2	1	3	OK, 1969
Shawnee	II	4	3	57	59	-4	1	3	4	TX, 1968
Oconee	I	2	2	48	56	-4	1	2	2	TX, 1989
Sioux	II	2	4	68	59	-1	1	1	2	TX, 1962
Cape Fear	I	3	2	55	55	0	2	3	2	NC, 1941
Stuart	II	5	2	50	47		4	2	1	MS, 1886
Wichita	II	1	5	52	60	0	3	4	4	TX, 1959
Cheyenne	I	1	3+	59	59	2	2	4	2	TX, 1970
Western	I	3	5+	53	55	4	2	2*	1	TX, 1924
GraKing	I	3	2	44	53	6	3	2	3	OK, 1930
Kiowa	II	2	2	46	58	7	2	3	4	TX, 1976
Desirable	I	4	3	50	53	8	2	3	3	MS, 1945
Houma	I	2	1	57	55	10	2	2	5	TX, 1989
Choctaw	II	3	2	45	59	12	3	3	2	TX, 1959

* Suitable for Western areas only where scab is not a problem

- Flowering: I = protandrous (early pollen), II= protogynous (late pollen)
- Precocity: 1 = earliest, 5= latest, -- to begin production after planting or propagating
- Scab: 1= least susceptible, 5= most susceptible to scab disease
- Nut size: nuts per pound
- % kernel: percent weight of kernel compared to total nut weight
- Nut maturity: number of days before (-) or after Stuart shucksplit (Oct. 16-Oct. 30) in northern OK
- Nut quality: kernel taste and appearance, ease of shelling (1:best)
- Tree quality: tree sturdiness, shape, disease/insect resistance, foliage color, etc. (1: best)
- Freeze tolerance: tolerance to early fall/late spring freezes, and cold winters (1: best)

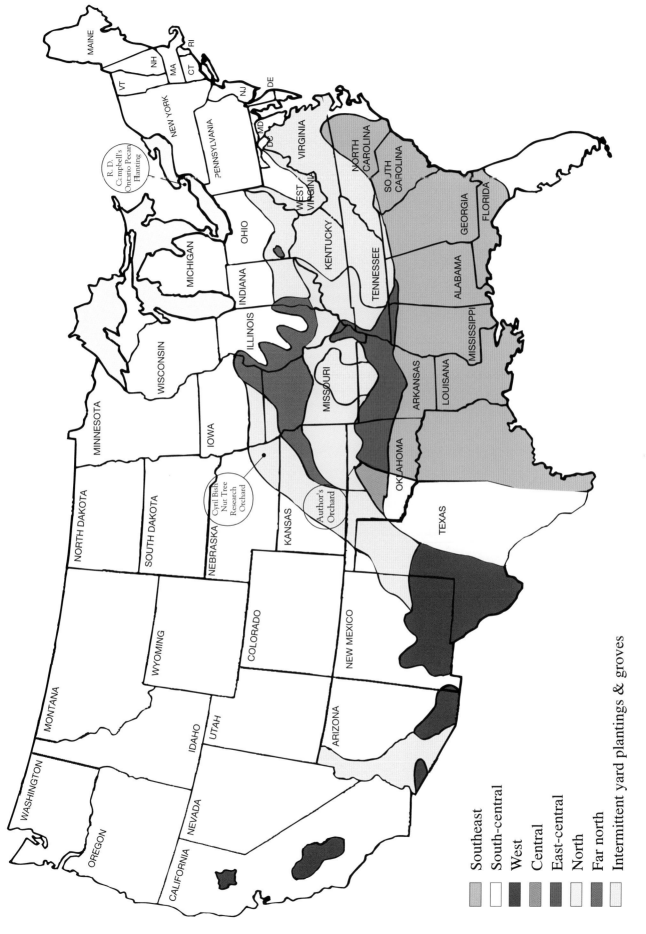

MAINE

NH

RI

VT

MA

CT

NEW YORK

NJ

DE

PENNSYLVANIA

MD

DC

VIRGINIA

WEST VIRGINIA

NORTH CAROLINA

SOUTH CAROLINA

GEORGIA

FLORIDA

OHIO

KENTUCKY

TENNESSEE

ALABAMA

MISSISSIPPI

MICHIGAN

INDIANA

ILLINOIS

MISSOURI

ARKANSAS

LOUISANA

WISCONSIN

R. D. Campbell's Ontario Pecan Planting

MINNESOTA

IOWA

OKLAHOMA

Cyril Bish Nut Tree Research Orchard

NEBRASKA

KANSAS

Author's Orchard

TEXAS

NORTH DAKOTA

SOUTH DAKOTA

MONTANA

WYOMING

COLORADO

NEW MEXICO

WASHINGTON

IDAHO

UTAH

ARIZONA

OREGON

NEVADA

CALIFORNIA

Southeast

South-central

West

Central

East-central

North

Far north

Intermittent yard plantings & groves

51

NUT ATTRIBUTES

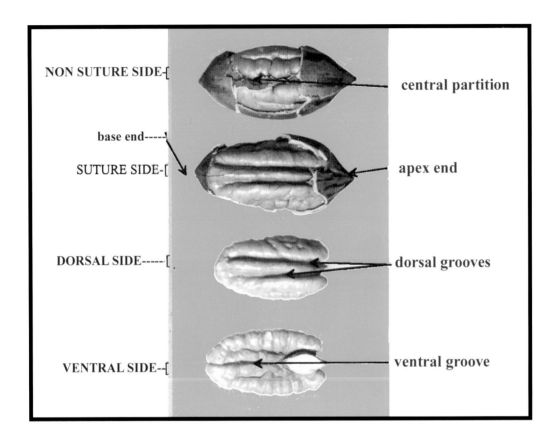

NON SUTURE SIDE-[central partition

base end----→   apex end

SUTURE SIDE-[

DORSAL SIDE-----[dorsal grooves

VENTRAL SIDE--[ventral groove

The following panels show the same orientation of views depicted in the above illustration. In other words, the non-suture view is on top, and the suture side is below it. Also, extreme care was exercised to maintain the exact scale of the nuts photographed. With true-to-scale pictures, the reader will have an easier time in making comparisons. Of course, nuts of the same cultivar will vary in size, depending on location and climatic factors.

Nut cluster photographs
Pictures of the nut plus the shuck (designated as the fruit) were taken after nut sizing, and for most cultivars, before shuck split. Nut cluster photos are not to scale.

Mature bud photographs
Buds for the different cultivars are sometimes distinctive, and can aid in cultivar identification. Pictures were taken during the dormant season when bud packages were fully developed.

OSAGE

Northern Cultivar

Origin: USDA-Brownwood, Texas, 1989
Tested as : 48-15-3, 'Major'-X-'Evers'
Pollen: I, precocity: 2, scab: 1
Nuts per pound: 85; % kernel: 54
Nut maturity: 31 days before 'Stuart'
6 before 'Colby'
Nut quality: 2; tree quality: 3
First northern cultivar developed in the USDA breeding program. Early nut maturity. Good flavor and shelling quality. Upright tree with a narrow canopy.

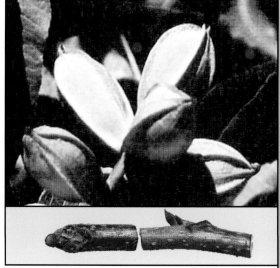

LUCAS

Ultra-northern Cultivar

Origin: seedling: Lucas, Ohio, 1965
Pollen: II; precocity: 2, scab: 1
Nuts per pound: 108; % kernel: 49
Nut maturity: 36 days before 'Stuart'
10 before 'Colby'
Nut quality: 2; tree quality: 3
Exceptionally early nut maturity. Good flavor and shelling quality. Willowy compact tree - producing small caliper scion wood. Tolerant to cold weather. Highly susceptible to yellow aphids.

COLBY

Northern Cultivar

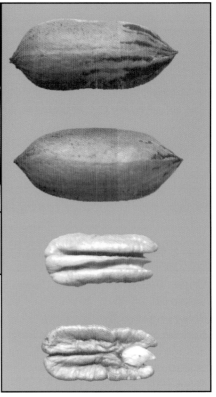

Origin: Clinton Co., Illinois, 1957
Pollen: II, precocity: 3, scab: 3+
Nuts per pound: 62; % kernel: 45
Maturity: 25 days before 'Stuart'
Nut quality: 4; tree quality: 2
Mediocre shelling quality. Resists freeze damage. A standard for northern cultivars. Foliage color tends to be light green. A popular seed nut. May require fungicide applications in humid climates.

PERUQUE

Northern Cultivar

Origin: seedling, Peruque, Missouri, 1953
Pollen: I, precocity: 2, scab: 3
Nuts per pound: 79; % kernel: 59-60+
Nut maturity: 27 days before 'Stuart'
Similar to 'Colby'
Nut quality: 2; tree quality: 2
Cold hardy. Consistent producer of quality nuts. Tree is somewhat compact, with large caliper, sturdy wood that resists ice and wind damage. Favored by crows and blue jays.

MAJOR

Northern Cultivar

Origin: seedling, Henderson, Kentucky, 1908
Pollen: I, precocity: 4, scab: 1
Nuts per pound: 79; % kernel: 49
Maturity: 15 days before 'Stuart'
10 after 'Colby'
Nut quality: 2; tree quality: 1
An old standard cultivar for northern areas.
Very cold hardy and sturdy tree which
produces a roundish nut which cracks well
manually. Doesn't align well in mechanical
cracking equipment.

POSEY

Northern Cultivar

Origin: seedling, Gibson Co., Indiana, 1911
Pollen: II, precocity: 4, scab: 1
Nuts per pound: 68; % kernel: 56
Nut maturity: 18 days before 'Stuart'
7 after 'Colby'
Nut quality: 2-3; tree quality: 1
Attractive yard tree with large dark green
leaves. Distinctive large thick husk. Kernels
darken quickly with age. Regular, shy
producer. Quality yard tree for northern areas.

GILES

Cold Tolerant

Origin: seedling, Chetopa, Kansas, 1930
Pollen: I, precocity: 2, scab: 3-4
Nuts per pound: 74; % kernel: 52
Nut maturity: 12 days before 'Stuart'
13 after 'Colby'
Nut quality: 3; tree quality: 4
Makes a cold hardy and vigorous rootstock.
Willowy tree structure that requires substantial
training. Often has a shriveled tip on one kernel.

HIRSCHI

Northern Cultivar

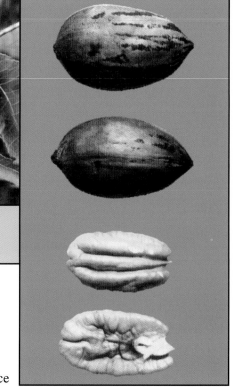

Origin: seedling, Rich Hill, Missouri, 1940
Pollen: I, precocity: 2, scab: 3
Nuts per pound: 72; % kernel: 50
Nut maturity: 22 days before 'Stuart'
 Similar to 'Colby'
Nut quality: 2; tree quality: 1
Attractive yard tree with tasty nuts. Resists ice
and wind damage. Moderate cracking qualities.
More resistant to bird depredation than
'Peruque'.

DOOLEY

Cold Tolerant

Origin: seedling, Okmulgee, Oklahoma, 1945
Pollen: I, precocity: 2, scab: 2-3
Nuts per pound: 79; % kernel: 47
Nut maturity: 11 days before 'Stuart'
Nut quality: 1; tree quality: 2
Kernel quality and ease of shelling are excellent, yielding perfect halves. Kernels are bright and smooth, with no adherence of shell material. Tree shows adequate disease resistance in most areas, and is attractive.

NORTON

Ultra-northern Cultivar

Origin: seedling, Clarksville, Missouri, 1912
Pollen: II, precocity: 4, scab: 2
Nuts per pound: 76; % kernel: 44
Nut maturity: 31 days before 'Stuart'
6 days before 'Colby'
Nut quality: 4; tree quality: 2
Very cold hardy, and enters dormancy very early - making it less susceptible to early fall freezes than many cultivars. Tree produces an attractive open canopy. Cracking qualities and kernel color are only fair.

WICHITA

Western Cultivar

Origin: USDA-Brownwood, Texas, 1959
Tested as 49-9-193, 'Halbert'-X-'Mahan'
Pollen: II, precocity: 1, scab: 5
Nuts per pound: 52; % kernel: 60
Nut maturity: Similar to 'Stuart'
Nut quality: 2-3; tree quality: 4
Kernels are plump and packed tightly in the
shell, yielding low percentages of perfect
halves. Requires extensive management,
but can be highly profitable in western dry
climates.

PAWNEE

Superior Standard
Cultivar
Suitable for northern
climates

Origin: USDA-Brownwood, Texas, 1984
63-16-125, 'Mohawk'-X-'Starking H. Giant'
Pollen: I, precocity: 3, scab: 2-3
Nuts per pound: 50; % kernel: 59
Nut maturity: 17 days before 'Stuart'
Nut quality: 2; tree quality: 2.5
Exceptionally early shuck split for a large nut.
My most profitable cultivar. A good selection
for both the yard and the orchard. Superior
performer for northern areas.

CHEYENNE

Standard Cultivar
Willowy, compact tree

Origin: USDA-Brownwood, Texas, 1970
Tested as : 42-13-2, 'Clark'-X-'Odom'
Pollen: I, precocity: 1, scab: 3-4
Nuts per pound: 59; % kernel: 59
Nut maturity: 2 days after 'Stuart'
Nut quality: 2; tree quality: 4
Nut kernels are wrinkled, and good quality.
Tree is compact and willowy, with a very open
canopy, thus subject to ice and wind damage.
Susceptible to yellow aphids.

WESTERN

Western Cultivar
Highly susceptible
to scab. Appropriate
for western, low
humidity areas.

Origin: seedling, San Saba, Texas, 1924
Pollen: I, precocity: 3, scab: 5
Nuts per pound: 53; % kernel: 55
Nut maturity: 4 days after 'Stuart'
Nut quality: 2; tree quality: 2
Standard cultivar for western, low humidity
areas. Popular as a yard tree in western areas.
Kernel quality is adequate, and tree has good
structure and resists wind and freeze damage.
Shell topology is rough and mottled.

SIOUX

Standard Cultivar
A standard for
nut quality.

Origin: USDA-Brownwood, Texas, 1962
Tested as: 43-4-6, 'Schley'-X-'Carmichael'
Pollen: II, precocity: 2, scab: 4
Nuts per pound: 68; % kernel: 59
Nut maturity: Similar to 'Stuart'
Nut quality: 1; tree quality: 1
Excellent yard tree with superior nut quality.
Nut size is small when compared with other
mid-season cultivars. Matures into one of the
largest/tallest improved variety trees.

SHAWNEE

Standard Cultivar

Origin: USDA-Brownwood, Texas, 1968
Tested as: 49-17-166, 'Schley'-X-'Barton'
Pollen: II, precocity: 4, scab: 3
Nuts per pound: 57; % kernel: 59
Nut maturity: 4 days before 'Stuart'
Nut quality: 2; tree quality: 3
Attractive light quality kernels that maintain
good quality in cold storage. Tree has an open
canopy, and is subject to ice and wind damage.
Sometimes lacks winter hardiness.

GRAKING

Standard Cultivar

Origin: seedling, Hugo, Oklahoma, 1930
Pollen: II, precocity: 3, scab: 2
Nuts per pound: 44 ; % kernel: 53
Nut maturity: 6 days after 'Stuart'
Nut quality: 3; tree quality: 2
One of 7 cultivars selected and released by O. S.
Gray. Nut quality is only fair, and kernels are
sometimes dry — at least in my opinion. Pistil
receptivity and pollen shed overlap — possibly
explaining its resistance to overproduction.

NAVAHO

Western Cultivar
Best suited to western
climates, highly
productive.

Origin: USDA-Brownwood, Texas, 1994
Tested as: 48-13-311-X-'Wichita'
48-13-311 is a 'Moore' -X-'Schley' cross
Pollen: I, precocity: 1, scab: 3
Nuts per pound: 61; % kernel: 63
Nut maturity: Similar to 'Stuart'
Nut quality: 2; tree quality: 2
Exceptionally fast growing precocious tree best
suited to western areas. Tree structure is strong
and sturdy, and has shown resistance to yellow
aphids. High production rates.

MARAMEC

Standard Cultivar

Origin: seedling, Maramec, Oklahoma, 1969
Pollen: II, precocity: 3, scab: 2+
Nuts per pound: 48; % kernel: 57
Nut maturity: 4 days before 'Stuart'
Nut quality: 2; tree quality: 1
Produces consistent crops of quality nuts.
Selected by Oklahoma State University in
1963, and was released in 1969. Tree is vigorous and sturdy, resisting ice and wind damage.
Yields perfect halves in mechanical crackers.

MOUNT

Standard Cultivar
A top quality
Oklahoma native.

Origin: seedling, Okmulgee, Oklahoma, 1966
Pollen: II, precocity: 3, scab: 1
Nuts per pound: 75; % kernel: 52
Nut maturity: 13 days before 'Stuart'
Nut quality: 2; tree quality: 1
Produces consistent crops of medium sized
nuts. Selected by Oklahoma State University in
1946, and was released in 1966. Tree is vigorous and sturdy, resisting ice and wind damage.
Cracking qualities and kernel flavor are good.

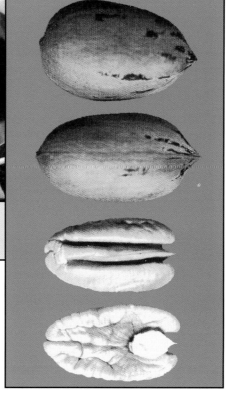

OCONEE

Standard Cultivar

Origin: USDA-Brownwood,Texas, 1989
Pollen: I, precocity: 2, scab: 2
Nuts per pound: 48; % kernel: 56
Nut maturity: similar to 'Stuart'
Nut quality: 2; tree quality: 2
Vigorous growing tree with adequate resistance to diseases. Tree has a moderately narrow canopy. Cracking/shelling properties are excellent either by hand or mechanically. Kernels are smooth with good color.

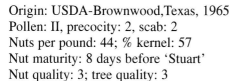

MOHAWK

Standard Cultivar

Largest USDA cultivar released to date.

Origin: USDA-Brownwood,Texas, 1965
Pollen: II, precocity: 2, scab: 2
Nuts per pound: 44; % kernel: 57
Nut maturity: 8 days before 'Stuart'
Nut quality: 3; tree quality: 3
Produces the largest nut in the USDA breeding program releases. Nuts are well filled in the first years of production, but the tree tends to overproduce as an older tree. Mechanical thinning is required produce a salable nut.

STUART

Standard Cultivar
Oldest widely planted
cultivar.

Origin: seedling, Pascagoula, Mississippi, 1886
Pollen: II, precocity: 5, scab: 2-3
Nuts per pound: 50; % kernel: 47
Nut maturity: Mid/late October in Oklahoma
Nut quality: 4; tree quality: 2
Best known and the oldest and most widely
planted named cultivar. People think of 'Stuart'
when "paper shell" pecans are mentioned, but
'Stuart is far from being a thin shelled pecan.
Tree is resistant to freeze and wind damage.

DESIRABLE

Standard Cultivar
A standard for southeast
USA.

Origin: Ocean Springs, Mississippi, 1945
'Success'-X-'Jewett'
Pollen: I, precocity: 4, scab: 3
Nuts per pound: 50; % kernel: 53
Nut maturity: 8 days after 'Stuart'
Nut quality: 2; tree quality: 3
Produces consistent crops of good quality
large pecans. Resistance to alternate bearing
and over production is superior to many other
cultivars. Requires fungicide applications in
humid areas.

CADDO

Standard Cultivar

Origin: USDA-Philema, Georgia, 1968
Tested as: Philema 1175, 'Brooks'-X-'Alley'
Pollen: I, precocity: 3, scab: 1-2
Nuts per pound: 70; % kernel: 56
Nut maturity: 6 days before 'Stuart'
Nut quality: 2; tree quality: 2
Quality performance on mature trees. Tree structure is sturdy and attractive — with good resistance to freeze and wind damage. A good all around yard or orchard cultivar selection.

CHOCTAW

Standard Cultivar
A good selection for areas with moderate humidity and a long growing season.

Origin: USDA-Brownwood, Texas, 1959
Tested as : 46-15-276, 'Success'-X-'Mahan'
Pollen: II, precocity: 3, scab: 2
Nuts per pound: 45; % kernel: 59
Nut maturity: 10 days after 'Stuart'
Nut quality: 2-3; tree quality: 3
Oldest USDA cultivar still recommended extensively for propagation. Leaf retention is extended, yet the tree appears resistant to freeze damage. Late ripening cultivar.

HOUMA

Standard Cultivar
Disease resistant
cultivar with late nut
maturity.

Origin: USDA-Brownwood, Texas, 1989
Tested as : 58-4-61, 'Desirable'-X-'Curtis'
Pollen: I, precocity: 2, scab: 1
Nuts per pound: 57; % kernel: 53
Nut maturity: 12 days after 'Stuart'
Nut quality: 1-2; tree quality: 2
Released for superior disease resistance and
good nut quality. Nut stores well in cold
storage. Young trees are highly susceptible to
freeze damage, and nut maturity is very late.

CAPE FEAR

Standard Cultivar

Origin: Schley seedling, Willard, NC, 1941
Pollen: I, precocity: 3, scab: 2
Nuts per pound: 55; % kernel: 55
Nut maturity: Similar to 'Stuart'
Nut quality: 2-3; tree quality: 3
Older popular variety in the southeast USA.
Tree is full and well branched, and goes dor-
mant relatively early. Leaf scorch is a serious
problem in some areas. Yields are consistent,
but quality is variable — especially on mature
trees.

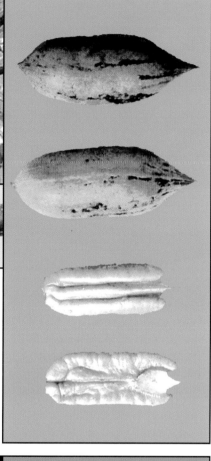

OK 642
(Moser)

Cold Tolerant Cultivar

Origin: Oklahoma,
Tested as Oklahoma 642
Pollen shed: II, precocity: 3, scab: 2
Nuts per pound 70, % kernel: 52
Nut maturity: 8 days before Stuart
Nut quality: 1.5, tree quality: 3
Fills well for an elongated nut, straw colored
kernels, growthy tree.

GREENRIVER

Cold Tolerant Cultivar

Origin: seedling, Henderson, Kentucky, 1911
Pollen shed: II, precocity: 4, scab: 1
Nuts per pound: 69, % kernel: 50
Nut maturity: 6 days before Stuart
Nut quality: 2, tree quality: 2
Dark green attractive foliage on a sturdy tree.
Green river does relatively well in southern
Kansas, northern Oklahoma, and is propagated
with success in KY, AR, and TN.

CHETOPA

Standard Cultivar

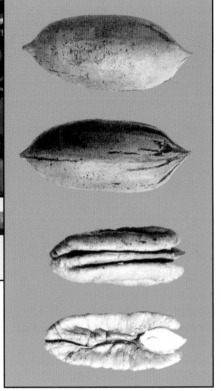

Origin: Chetopa, Kansas, 1995
Seedling, tested as K-112
Pollen shed II, precocity: 3, scab: 2
Nuts per pound: 65, % kernel: 54
Nut maturity: similar to 'Stuart'
Nut quality: 2, tree quality: 2
Flavorful kernels, narrow dorsal grooves

POINTE COUPEE #2
(PCOU-2)

Standard Cultivar

Origin: seedling, Pointe Coupee Parish, LA
Nuts per pound: 60, % kernel: 52
Pollen shed: II, precocity: 3, scab: 2
Nut maturity: similar to 'Stuart'
Nut quality: 2, tree quality: 2.5
Scab resistance appears to be inadequate for
low input orchards in the southeast USA.

NACONO

Standard Cultivar

Origin: USDA Brownwood, Texas, 2000
Tested as 74-5-55, 'Cheyenne'-x-'Sioux'
Pollen shed: II, precocity: 3, scab: ~2.5
Nut quality: 1, tree quality: 1.5
Nuts per pound: 44, % kernel: 56
Nut maturity: 4 days before 'Stuart'
Nut quality is excellent, with bright straw
colored kernels and excellent flavor. Tree
structure and foliage are very good and
disease resistance is adequate in most areas.

HOPI

Western Cultivar

Origin: USDA, Brownwood, Texas, 1999
Tested as: 39-5-50, 'Schley'-x- 'McCulley'
Pollen shed: II, precocity: 3, scab: 4
Nuts per pound: 46, % kernel: 62
Nut maturity: late
Nut quality: 1, tree quality: 2
'Hopi' has been under evaluation since 1939.
Primarily suited for western states with lower
humidity levels. Produces moderate yields of
high quality nuts.

KANZA

Standard Cultivar

Cold Tolerant

Origin: USDA Brownwood, Texas, 1996
Tested as 55-11-11, 'Major'-x-'Shoshoni'
pollen shed II, precocity: 3, scab: 1.5
Nuts per pound: 70, % kernel: 54
Nut maturity: 11 days earlier than Stuart
Nut quality: 1, tree quality: 1
Very good nut quality, shells into perfect
halves, resists freeze damage; pollenizes
'Pawnee.'

CREEK

Standard Cultivar

Disease Resistant

Origin: USDA Brownwood, Texas, 1996
Tested as 61-6-67, 'Mohawk'-x-'Starking H. G.'
Pollen shed: I, precocity: 2, scab: 1
Nuts per pound: 50, % kernel: 54
Nut maturity: 2 days earlier than Stuart
Nut quality: 3, tree quality: 2.5
Wide dorsal groves, produces young and
heavy; resists scab disease; susceptible to
freeze damage after a heavy crop.

SALOPEK

Western Cultivar

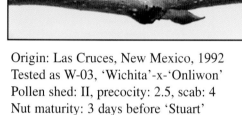

Origin: Las Cruces, New Mexico, 1992
Tested as W-03, 'Wichita'-x-'Onliwon'
Pollen shed: II, precocity: 2.5, scab: 4
Nut maturity: 3 days before 'Stuart'
Nut quality: 2.5, Tree quality: 3
Nuts per pound: 54, percent kernel: 60
Suitable for lower humidity climates

APACHE

Western Cultivar

Used as a seed nut

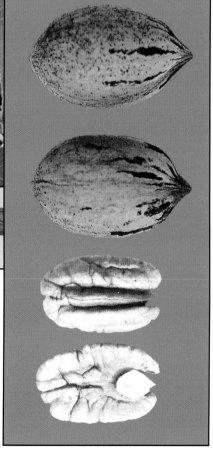

Origin: USDA Brownwood, TX, 1962
Tested as: 40-4-17, 'Burkett'-x-'Schley'
Pollen shed: II, precocity: 3, scab: 5
Nuts per pound: 55, % kernel: 58
Nut maturity: 10 days after Stuart
Nut quality: 2, tree quality: 2 (western areas)
Frequently used as a seed nut in western
areas. A good quality nut when scab can be
controlled.

FORKERT

Standard Cultivar

Origin: Ocean Springs, MS, ~1915
'Success'-x-'Schley'
Pollen shed: II, precocity: 2, scab: 3
Nuts per pound: 50, % kernel: 62
Nut quality: 1, tree quality: 2
Nut maturity: 3 days before 'Stuart'
Rough shell topography, thin shell.
Recommended in several states and
is increasing in popularity.

MORELAND

Standard Cultivar
Adequate scab
resistance for most areas.

Origin: 'Schley'? seedling, Powhatan, LA, 1945
Pollen shed: II, precocity: 3, scab: 2
Nuts per pound: 57, % kernel: 56
Nut maturity: 4 days after 'Stuart'
Nut quality: 2, tree quality: 3
Recommended in several southeastern states;
sometimes kernels are wrinkled but have good
flavor and color. Inshell nut has a somewhat
unique shape and color.

CANDY

Standard Cultivar

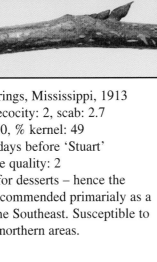

Origin: Ocean Springs, Mississippi, 1913
Pollen shed II, precocity: 2, scab: 2.7
Nuts per pound: 70, % kernel: 49
Nut maturity: 10 days before 'Stuart'
Nut quality: 1, tree quality: 2
Used as a topper for desserts – hence the name 'Candy.' Recommended primarialy as a yard planting in the Southeast. Susceptible to freeze damage in northern areas.

ELLIOTT

(Elliot)

Standard Cultivar
Standard for scab and disease resistance.

Origin: seedling, Milton Florida, 1925
Pollen shed: II, precocity: 2, scab: 1-S
Nuts per pound: 71, % kernel: 54
Nut maturity: 3 days before 'Stuart'
Nut quality: 1, tree quality: 2
Very early bud break; susceptible to spring freezes. Often used as a southern rootstock. Highly resistant to scab disease, often referenced as a standard for disease resistance. Recommended yard tree in the Southeast.

Additional scab ratings for highly resistant cultivars:

1-S (superior)

1-E (excellent)

1-G (very good)

See page 49 for further information.

SUMNER

Standard Cultivar

Origin: Tift County, Georgia, 1932
Pollen shed: II, precocity: 2, scab: 1-G
Nuts per pound: 49, % kernel: 54
Nut maturity: 13 days after 'Stuart'
Nut quality: 3, tree quality: 2
'Sumner' is a prolific bearer of late maturing nuts. The tree is upright with strong branching, and has attractive foliage. Scab resistance is good, so the tree is popular in southeastern areas with a long growing season.

BARTON

Standard Cultivar
Disease resistant

Origin: USDA Brownwood, Texas, 1953
Tested as 37-3-20, 'Moore'-x-'Success'
Pollen shed: I, precocity: 3, scab: 1
Nuts per pound: 55, % kernel: 57
Nut maturity: 10 days before 'Stuart'
Nut quality: 2, tree quality: 2
The earliest USDA release, and the only USDA cultivar not named after a Native American tribe. One of the most scab resistant cultivars. Overbears as an older tree; requires thinning.

JENKINS

Standard Cultivar
Highly disease resistant.

Origin: seedling, Rena Lara, Mississippi
Pollen shed: II, scab resistance: 1-S
Precocity: 3.5, nuts per pound: 54,
% kernel: 56, nut maturity: similar to 'Stuart'
nut quality: 3, tree quality: 2
No longer recommended for low input
orchards, 'Jenkins' has shown susceptibility to
zonate leaf spot, and kernels may develop fuzz
under stressed conditions.

GLORIA GRANDE

Origin: 'Stuart'? Sdlg., Orangeburg, SC, 1923
Pollen shed: 2, precocity: 4, scab: 1-2
Nuts per pound: 46, % kernel: 47
Nut maturity: 5 days after 'Stuart'
Nut quality: 4, tree quality: 2
Sometimes referenced as "improved Stuart."
Nut quality and crackability exceed 'Stuart',
and scab resistance is also better. Good tree
structure. Disease and freeze resistance
are good, but nut quality is only mediocre.

McMILLAN

Standard Cultivar
Good disease resistance.

Origin: seedling, Baldwin County, Alabama
Nuts per pound: 59, % kernel: 51
Pollen Shed: I, scab resistance: 1-S
Nut maturity: similar to 'Stuart'
Nut quality: 2.5, Tree quality: 2
Precocity: 2.5
Recommended for low input orchards.

SYRUP MILL

Standard Cultivar
Good disease resistance.

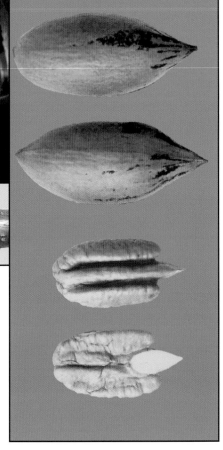

Origin: seedling, Mobile County. Alabama
Nuts per pound: 45, % kernel: 47
Nut quality: 2, Tree quality: 2
Pollen shed: I, precocity: 3
Scab resistance: 1-2
Nut maturity: 7 days after 'Stuart'
Good cracking qualities, marginal percent
kernel. Not recommended for low input
orchards.

GAFFORD

Standard Cultivar
Good disease resistance.

Origin: seedling, Butler County, Alabama
Pollen shed: I, scab resistance: 1-S
Nuts per pound: 56, % kernel: 52
Nut quality: 2.5, Tree quality: 1
Nut maturity: similar to 'Stuart'
Precocity: 3
Suitable for low input orchards. Nut maturity
is generally early enough for sites where
'Stuart' ripens.

CARTER

Standard Cultivar
Good disease resistance.

Origin: seedling, Jackson County, MS.
Nuts per pound: 49, % kernel: 49
Pollen Shed: II, Scab resistance: excellent
Nut quality: 3, Tree quality: 3
Nut Maturity: similar to 'Stuart'
Precocity: 4
Suitable for low input orchards, and
susceptible to freeze injury.

WACO

Standard Cultivar
Newest USDA release

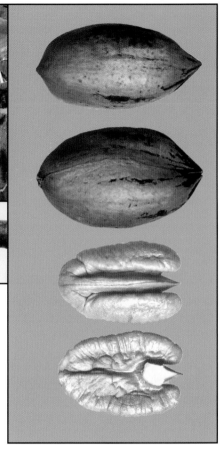

Origin: USDA Brownwood, Texas, 2005
Tested as 75-5-6, 'Cheyenne'-x-'Sioux'
Pollen shed: I, precocity: 2, scab: ~2.5
Nut quality: 1, tree quality: 1.5
Nuts per pound: 45, % kernel: 56
Shuck split: similar to 'Stuart'
Bright straw colored kernels with excellent
flavor. Tree has large, attractive leaves.

EXCEL
(Patent Pending)

Standard Cultivar
Disease resistant

Origin: Blackshear, Georgia
Nuts per pound ~ 45, % kernel: 50
Pollen shed: II
Dr. Bill Goff recently indicated that 'Excel',
currently under evaluation at the Coastal Plain
Experiment Station in Tifton, Georgia, has
many of the attributes he deems necessary
for pecan culture in the Southeast. These
attributes include superior scab resistance,
early nut maturity, good kernel quality, and
sturdy tree structure. 'Excel' kernels are also
reported to maintain good flavor and color in
cold storage. 'Excel' is reported to be one of
the few cultivars with large nut size and superior scab resistance. Of course, resistance to
scab varies with time and resistance is subject
to mutation of the different scab races. It is
currently recommended for trial plantings.
Additional information on 'Excel', and other
cultivars can be found at the University of
Georgia website:
www.cpes.peachnet.edu/pecan/

STANDARD CULTIVARS

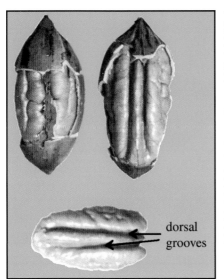

PICTURE LAYOUT: (left)
For all plates of this format:
left view: non-suture side
right view: suture side
lower kernel view: dorsal side

Squirrel (right)
(*Squirrel's delight*)
Origin: San Saba seedling, San Saba,
Texas, ~1930,
Pollen shed: I, precocity: 2, scab: 5
Nuts per pound: 56, % kernel: 56
Nut maturity: 9 days before 'Stuart,'
Nut quality: 2.5
Flavorful nut when scab is controlled.

dorsal
grooves

GraTex (left)
Origin: Arlington, Texas, 1962
'Ideal'-x-'Success'
Pollen shed: II, precocity: 4, scab: 4
Nuts per pound: 52, % kernel: 62, nut quality: 2
Nut maturity: similar to 'Stuart', tree quality: 4
Willowy, poor structured tree erroneously report-
ed in some literature as having early nut maturity.

Sullivan (right)
Origin: Las Cruces, NM, 1983
'Stuart'-x-'Nugget'
Pollen shed: II, precocity: 3, scab: 3.5
Nuts per pound: 66, % kernel: 56, nut quality: 2
Nut maturity: 7 days before 'Stuart'
A New Mexico release with early nut maturity
(compared with other western cultivars).
Bred for higher elevations.

Hodge (left)
Seedling, Clark Co., Illinois, 1893
pollen shed: 2, precocity: 4, scab: 2-3
nuts per pound: 72, % kernel: 44
nut quality: 3, tree quality: 3
shuck split: 8 days after 'Colby'
First recognized northern cultivar

Prilop (right)
Seedling, Lavaca Co., Texas
pollen shed: I, % kernel: 57
nuts per pound: 110, reported at 78
precocity: 3-4, scab: 1-2
Nut maturity: similar to 'Stuart'
Nut quality: 1, tree quality: 2
Small high quality nut; matures late

Jackson (left), seedling
Ocean Springs, MS, 1917
Nuts per pound: 43
% kernel: 60, pollen shed: II
Precocity: 4, scab: 2
Nut quality: 1, tree quality: 2
Shuck split: similar to 'Stuart'
High quality nut/tree, shy yield.

Podsednik (right) seedling,
Arlington, Texas
Nuts per pound: 22,
% kernel: 44, pollen shed: I,
Precocity: 3, scab: 2.5
Nut quality: 4, tree quality: 2
Shuck split: similar to 'Stuart'
Thought to be the largest nut,
but often poor in quality.

Burkett (left) - seedling
Clyde Texas, 1911
Nuts per pound: 44,
% kernel: 55
Pollen shed: II, precocity: 2
Scab: 5, susceptible to rosette
Nut quality: 2, tree quality: 4
Speckled kernel
Shuck split: 7 days after 'Stuart'
Old unique western cultivar.

Farley (right)
Jackson Co, FL, ~1925
Nuts per pound: 59
% kernel: 53
Pollen shed: II
Precocity: 5, scab: 2
Shuck split: late, shy yield

Melrose (left)
Hanna, LA, 1979
Nuts per pound: 55
% kernel: 55 pollen shed: II,
Precocity: 3 scab: 1-2
Nut quality: 2, tree quality: 2
Shuck split: 4 days after
'Stuart'

Older and Other Standard Cultivars

Cultivars listed here were selected for a number of reasons, including nut size, disease resistance, tree quality, personal preference, etc. Deemed by some growers as now obsolete, many of these cultivars are still popular in various regions of the country. For example, a few 'Podsednik' trees will likely frequent yards and orchards as long as pecan trees exist. Although often a disappointment when kernel quality is considered, many orchardist and home owners are enthralled by 'Podsednik' with its large nut size. 'Burkett' is still popular because of its unique kernel flavor and appearance. Similarly, most other cultivars have their own strengths, weaknesses, and unique appealing properties.

OKLAHOMA CULTIVARS

Oklahoma Releases

With the exception of 'Cowley', the five cultivars shown on this page were released as pecans for the <u>shelling trade</u>. Professor Herman Hinrichs played an essential role in Oklahoma's pecan industry, and directed an extensive evaluation from 1946-78 of Oklahoma's best seedling pecans. Seven cultivars were released as a result of the evaluation. The two most recognized cultivars from the program are 'Mount' and 'Maramec', which are described and illustrated on page 62.

Gormely (right)
Origin: Okemah, OK, 1966
Tested as # 463
Pollen shed: II, precocity: 3
Scab rating: 1, nuts per pound: 88
% kernel: 49
Shuck split: 17 days before 'Stuart'
Nut quality 2, tree quality: 1
One of the more scab resistant
Oklahoma varieties; a variety preferred
by black aphids.

Hayes (left)
Origin: Oklahoma
Pollen shed: II, precocity: 4
Scab rating: 2.5,
Nuts per pound: 90, % kernel: 58
Shuck split: 13 days before 'Stuart'
Nut quality: 2, Tree quality: 2.5

Patrick (right)
Origin: Claremore, Oklahoma
Shuck split: 14 days before 'Stuart'
Pollen shed: II, precocity: 4
Nuts per pound: 110, % kernel: 60+
Nut quality: 1, tree quality: 3
Discovered by Floyd A. Patrick.

Oakla (left)
Origin: Oklahoma
Tested as # 512
Nuts per pound: 90, % kernel: 50
Nut quality: 1, tree quality: 2

Cowley (right)
Tested as # 60L2
Nuts per pound: 50
Kernel quality: usually very poor on
mature trees.
Author opinion: not recommended for
propagation.

OTHER CULTIVARS

Silverback
Origin: Okmulgee, Oklahoma, mid-1990's
Nuts per pound: 36, % kernel: 52
Pollen shed: II, precocity: 3, scab: 1.5
Shuck split: 5 days after Stuart
Recently offered by Stark Brothers Nursery
as: 'Starking Southern Giant.'

Fritz Flat
Seedling, New Boston area, Illinois
Nuts per pound: 78, % kernel: 48
Nut maturity: similar to 'Colby'
Precocious cultivar, but nut quality
is mediocre and nut maturity is too
late for ultra-northern regions.

Carlson Crow
New Boston area, Illinois
Nuts per pound: 98, % kernel: 47
No other data

Shoals West
Origin: Chilicothie, Missouri
Pollen shed: I
Nuts per pound: 101, % kernel: 44
Shuck split: 7 days before 'Colby'

IN QUEST OF BETTER CULTIVARS

Seeking out improved cultivars has been an ongoing goal of mankind. In pecans, documentation indicates that individuals have evaluated and named select seedlings since the nineteenth century, and likely before. 'Stuart' was discovered in Pascagoula, Mississippi in 1886. Other select seedlings, such as 'Posey', 'Peruque', 'Major', and others were selected, many by amateur horticulturists, because of unique properties that the cultivars possessed. Controlled pollination was also initiated by individuals, attempting to breed cultivars with known genetic factors from both the male and female parents.

The USDA initiated an organized breeding program in 1930. Since then, tens of thousands of controlled crosses have been made, and 25 cultivars have been released for propagation.

Evaluation of seedling pecans continues both by pecan specialists, and by individuals. Efforts by pecan specialist Dr. Bill Goff, Auburn University, have resulted in the identification of several cultivars with exceptional disease resistance, and other redeeming qualities. 'Jenkins', 'Gafford', 'Syrup Mill', 'Mc Millan', and 'Carter' are examples of these cultivars. Pecan and Nut Grower Associations hold nut contests to locate seedling pecans with superior qualities.

The 'Biggs' Pecan

'Biggs' was discovered by the Biggs family in Grandbury, Texas. The original tree was moved to Hobbs, New Mexico, at the home of Faye Capps, Biggs' granddaughter. Paul Muhle, a knowledgeable pecan grower from Rising Star, Texas, has propagated the 'Biggs' variety, and entered pecan samples in county pecan shows where it won "best of show."

The 'Pounds' Pecan

Another example is the discovery of the 'Pounds' pecan in Gentryville, Indiana. The 'Pounds' pecan grew under a 'Major' tree at the home of Leon "Doc" Pounds and was later transplanted to the home of Jerry Lehman, a well known persimmon and nut grower from Terre Haute, Indiana. Mr. Lehman has evaluated the pecan since the mid 1980's, and recent-

ly provided scion wood to establish the cultivar in my orchard. Sample pecans provided by Mr. Lehman indicate better than average quality and size for a northern cultivar. The tree also has an attractive shape and foliage, with apparent resistance to scab and other diseases.

I always enjoy finding out about the "man – or woman" behind the pecan. Like myself, other individuals enjoy seeking Nature's specialties. We can always hope for something unique on our own farm or in our backyard. Leon Pounds was such a person. As a point of interest, Leon was called "Doc" because he used to own the Rockport Sanitary Pottery (they made plumbing fixtures), and whenever anyone got hurt on the job, Leon would nurse their cuts, etc. and if need be take them to the local doctor. Thus the name "Doc" just stuck with him. Leon was a member of the Nut Growers Associations in Indiana and Kentucky. Leon loved to work with his nut trees, and experimented with different tree species and grafting techniques. Like all of us, some experiments were very successful and some were not. According to his grandson, Leon, and granddaughter, Jackie, the picture shown below captures the true Leon. He looked stern when deep in thought but had a smile that was infectious. "Doc" Pounds was born on September 6, 1907, and left this earth on January 24, 2003. We will miss Leon and others like him who contributed unselfishly to advances in plant science.

The 'Maramec' Pecan

Oklahoma Professor Herman Hinrichs initiated a project in 1946 to seek out Oklahoma's best seedling pecans. An emphasis was placed on pecans for the shelling trade. Seven cultivars were identified and released for propagation. Although most were smaller nuts with good kernel content and quality, 'Maramec', a large, thin shelled pecan was identified and released. It has become one of the most popular pecans in Oklahoma, having good size and excellent quality. 'Maramec,' and other Oklahoma releases are described on pages 62 and 81. 'Maramec' originated in Maramec, Oklahoma, and the 'Maramec' parent seedling still stands in it's original location.

It is reported that the nut that produced the 'Maramec' tree was obtained by Ms. Rutha Lewis Willard, who brought several large thin shelled nuts (thought to be 'Mahan') from another state and gave them to her daughter, Emma Charlton. Dr. Glen "Cat" Taylor reports from past discussions with Dr. Hinrichs that Ms. Charlton planted several of the nuts close to her porch by poking holes in the ground with her cane. One grew, prospered, and produced large, thin shelled, quality nuts on an attractive tree. After considering a name for the pecan, Ms. Charlton's daughter indicated that the pecan should be named after the "sleepy little town" of Maramec, Oklahoma -- rather than after her mother.

Ms. Gladys Kitchens, a Pawnee County, Oklahoma, historian, reports that Rutha and Enoch Willard came to Pawnee County from Missouri about 1901. Rutha was born in Tennessee. Emma was the oldest child of the family and married Anson/ Amous Charlton about 1908. Rutha Willard was born April 14, 1870, and died June 8,

1961. She is interred at the Maramec, Oklahoma Cemetery. Emma Charlton was born March 28, 1891, and died April 19, 1980.

'Maramec' was released by Oklahoma State University in 1969. Although Ms. Charlton lived to see the release and propagation of 'Maramec,' Ms. Willard never knew of her contribution to the pecan industry.

Leon "Doc" Pounds

The USDA Pecan Breeding and Genetics Research Worksite near College Station, Texas.

Shown above are Dr. Tommy Thompson (right) and Dr. L. J. Grauke, who direct ongoing efforts to breed and evaluate new pecan cultivars. This worksite, and a Brownwood, Texas, site also hold the National Clonal Germplasm Repository for pecan, hickory, and hican. To date, twenty-five pecan cultivars have been released to the pecan industry.

Ms. Rutha Lewis Willard

EXPERIMENTAL/PROMISING CULTIVARS

Faith (left)
Origin: Arkansas City, Kansas,
'Mohawk' seedling, 1996
Pollen shed: I, precocity: 3, scab: 3
Nuts per pound: 51, % kernel: 57
Shuck split: similar to 'Pawnee'
Nut quality: 2, tree quality: 3
Nut and tree resemble 'Pawnee.'

Clark II (right)
Origin: USDA, Brownwood, Texas
Selected in Albany, Georgia
Nuts per pound: 48, % kernel: 54,
Nut quality: 2, tree quality: 2
Pollen shed: II, precocity: 3, scab: 2
Shuck split: 8 days before 'Stuart'
Unknown USDA clone, named after
Bill Clark, past manager of the
Ducker Plantation.

Jayhawk
Origin: 'Giles' seedling, Kansas
Pollen shed: II,
Precocity: 3, scab: 2
68 nuts per pound, % kernel: 52
Shuck split: similar to 'Giles'

Biggs
Origin: Granbury, Texas, ~1955
Seedling
Pollen shed: I, precocity: 2, scab: 3,
Nut quality: 2, tree quality: 4
Nuts per pound: 57, % kernel: 57
Nut maturity: 5 days after 'Stuart'
Excellent crackability, placed first in
county shows, and was awarded best
seedling nut in Texas state shows.
Further information is listed on page
83.

Pounds
Origin: Gentryville, Indiana, 1983
'Major' seedling
Pollen shed: I, precocity: 3-4
Scab resistance: good
Nuts per pound: 79, % kernel: 47
Shuck split: similar to 'Major'
Selected by Leon Pounds, and
evaluated by Jerry Lehman, Terre
Haute, Indiana.
Further information is listed
on page 83.

NORTHERN AND ULTRA – NORTHERN CULTIVAR CATEGORIES

The following cultivar selections are suited for northern, and in some cases, higher elevation climates. Nuts are typically smaller in size, and have thicker shells than standard cultivars shown in the previous section. Also in many cases, northern/ultra-northern cultivars are slower to come into production than standard cultivars. They will, however, survive and produce a crop in northern geographical areas. In the long haul, their standard cultivar counterparts will typically succumb to these cold conditions.

Top rated ultra-northern cultivars

These cultivars are shown on the first pages and displayed in the long format (two cultivars per page). In other words, these are some of the better known and more widely evaluated varieties. Nut sizes are small to medium, but crops will often ripen before the first fall freeze as far north as Agricultural Zone 4B. Trees will also usually survive the low temperatures if proper cultural practices are followed. Kernel flavor is good, and appearance is attractive. Cracking quality of the nuts is good, yielding perfect halves on a regular basis.

Category 1 – Early ripening cultivars with superior qualities

This category includes cultivars that have very early nut maturity, trees withstanding conditions as far north as Agricultural Zone 4, and produce crops that ripen frequently. Some selections are likely as good as the top rated cultivars, but have yet to be tested adequately. Nuts typically yield flavorful kernels, and cracking quality is good.

Category 2 – Early ripening cultivars with good qualities

This category represents selections that are somewhat less cold hardy than those listed above, and require on the average, a longer growing season for the crop to ripen. Most have been tested widely enough that their strengths and weaknesses are documented.

Category 3 – Sub-northern cultivars

This category includes cultivars that are usually successful in Agricultural Zone 6, and may live and produce nuts in Zone 5 on a less regular basis. Kernel properties and cracking qualities are typically good.

Category 4 – Poor Performers

This category includes cultivars which, based on my observations and opinions, have few redeeming qualities. Nut maturity dates, disease resistance, nut size, and tree characteristics deem these cultivars as poor selections for propagation.

JAMES

Northern to
Ultra-Northern Cultivar

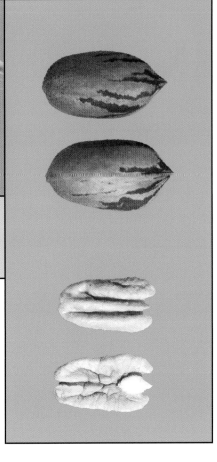

Origin: Seedling, Brunswick, MO, 19xx
Pollen shed: I, precocity: 3, scab: 2
Nuts per pound: 92, % kernel: 51
Nut maturity: 30 days before 'Stuart'
4 days before 'Colby', nut quality: 1,
Tree quality: 2
One of the better hardy pecans that will
survive and produce in southern Nebraska,
northern Missouri and similar climates.

STARKING HARDY GIANT

Ultra-Northern Cultivar

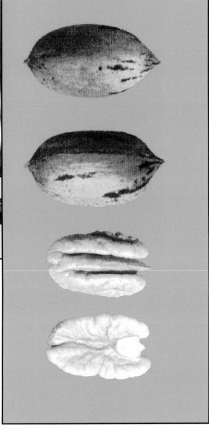

Origin: Seedling, Brunswick, MO, 1950
Pollen shed: I, precocity: 2, scab: 3.5
Nuts per pound: 75, shelling percent: 56
Nut maturity: 35 days before 'Stuart'
9 days before 'Colby', nut quality: 2.5,
Tree quality: 3
Exceptionally large and thin shelled for a nut
with such early maturity. Selected parent for
two released USDA cultivars. Scabs.

MULLAHY

Ultra-Northern Cultivar

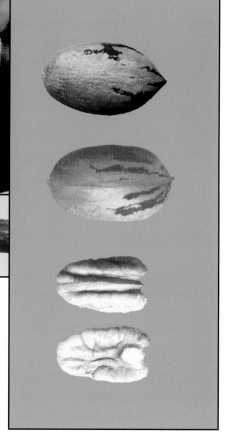

Origin: Seedling, Burlington, IA,
Pollen shed: II, precocity: 3, scab: 3
Nuts per pound: 79, % kernel: 49
Nut maturity: 33 days before 'Stuart'
7 days before 'Colby', nut quality: 2,
Tree quality: 2
One of the larger nut sizes of the ultra-north-
ern class. Shells into perfect halves.

DUMBELL LAKE

Best selection

Confusion has existed between the
two selections collected at Dumbell
Lake, near Burlington, Iowa.
Originally enumerated as 'Dumbell
Lake Large' and 'Dumbell Lake
Small,' Gary Fernald, who observed
the original trees, indicates that
"Large" relates to a large mature tree.
"Small" relates to a younger, smaller
tree. Since the scion wood was originally distributed, I have observed
what appears to be several ambiguities in the identification of the two
cultivars in different locations. I definitely have two different cultivars
established in my orchard, and one is
definitely better than the other in
both nut quality, and precocity.
Displayed here is the better of the
two cultivars. The other cultivar is
shown later in this chapter and is
labeled 'Dumbell Lake- other.' The
cultivar displayed here shows promise as a superior ultra-northern cultivar; the other selection is mediocre.

Origin: Seedling, Burlington, IA, 1980s
Pollen shed: I, precocity: 3, scab: 2
Nuts per pound: 89, % kernel: 47
Nut maturity: 32 days before 'Stuart'
6 days before 'Colby', nut quality: 2,
Tree quality: 2
Good kernel color and cracking qualities.
Dumbell Lake is a "pond" north of Burlington,
IA. Passports for the two Dumbell Lake selec-
tions are often switched.

GIBSON

Ultra-Northern Cultivar

Origin: New Boston, IL
Precocity: 4, scab: 2, pollen shed: I
Nuts per pound: 128, % kernel: 50
Nut maturity: 3 days before 'Colby'
Nut quality: 2, tree quality: 2
Prolific producer of good quality small nuts.
Cracking quality is good.

GREEN ISLAND BEAVER
(Cornfield)

Ultra-Northern Cultivar

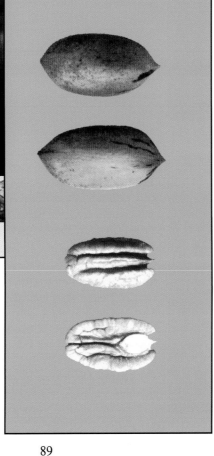

Origin: Green Island, IA
Pollen shed: II, nuts per pound: 152,
% kernel: 46,
Nut maturity: 16 days before 'Colby'
Nut quality: 1, tree quality: 2
Extremely early and cold hardy. Leaf drop is
very early, thus this cultivar is resistant to
early fall freezes. Cracking quality is good,
however, nut size if very small.

Warren #346 (left)
Origin: Wheeling, MO
Pollen Shed: II, scab: 1
Nuts per pound: 79, % kernel: 50
Shucksplit: 'Colby' - 21
Nut quality: 2, tree quality: 3
Winter hardy, very early shucksplit

Martzahn (right)
Origin: Burlington, IA, 1925
Pollen shed: II, scab: 1
Nuts per pound: 135, % kernel: 47
Shucksplit: 'Colby'-19
Nut quality: 4, tree quality: 2
Winter hardy, small marginal nut.

Snaps Early (left)
Origin: Pleasant Creek, IA
Pollen Shed: I , scab: 1
Nuts per pound: 127, % kernel: 50
Shucksplit: 'Colby'-17
Nut quality: 2.5, tree quality: 2
Cold hardy, early nut maturity

Carlson 3 (right)
Origin: New Boston, IL
Pollen shed: ?, scab: 2
Nuts per pound: 105, %kernel: 48
Shucksplit: 'Colby' - 17
Nut quality: 2, tree quality: 2
Productive early maturing cultivar.

Lucas (left)
See page 53 for description. One of the better ultra-northern cultivars. Nuts shown here are from my planting near Ponca City, Oklahoma, yielding 91 per pound.

Campbell NC4 (right)
Origin: Niagra area, Ontario
Pollen shed: I, scab: 2
Nuts per pound: 68, % kernel: 54
Shucksplit: 'Colby' - 8
Nut quality: 2, tree quality: 2
Cold hardy. One of the larger ultra-northern varieties, shy bearer.

NORTHERN CULTIVARS – CATEGORY 2

Canton (left)
Origin: Canton, MO
Pollen shed: I, scab: 2
Nuts per pound: 67, % kernel: 48
Nut quality: 3, tree quality: 2
Shuck split: 3 days before 'Colby'

Deerstand (right)
Origin: Burlington, IA area
Nuts per pound: 101,% kernel: 52
Shuck split: 8 days before 'Colby'
Nut quality: 2, tree quality: 2
Good cracking qualities.

Devore (left)
Origin: Wapello, IA, 1978
Pollen shed: II , scab: 2
Nuts per pound: 116, % kernel: 49
Nut quality: 3, tree quality: 2
Shuck split: 2 days before 'Colby'
Cold-hardy tree; used as a northern
rootstock.

Fisher (right)
Origin: New Memphis, IL, 1938
Nuts per pound: 79, % kernel: 46
Scab: 2
Shuck split: 4 days before 'Colby'
Good flavor and cracking quality

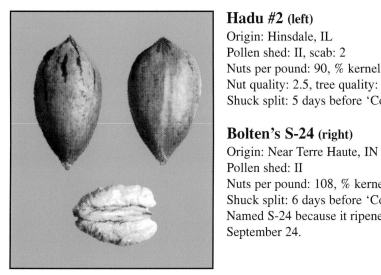

Hadu #2 (left)
Origin: Hinsdale, IL
Pollen shed: II, scab: 2
Nuts per pound: 90, % kernel: 50
Nut quality: 2.5, tree quality: 2
Shuck split: 5 days before 'Colby'

Bolten's S-24 (right)
Origin: Near Terre Haute, IN
Pollen shed: II
Nuts per pound: 108, % kernel: 48
Shuck split: 6 days before 'Colby'
Named S-24 because it ripened on
September 24.

Yates 152 (left)
Origin: Chrisney, Indiana, ~1990
'Major' seedling ('Posey' ? pollen)
Pollen shed — likely protogynous
Nuts per pound: 58, % kernel: 63
Propagated by Ed Yates

Goosepond (right)
Origin: Keytesville, Missouri,
Scab: 2, pollen shed: II
Nuts per pound: 68, % kernel: 48
Shuck split: 7 days after Colby
Nut quality: 2, tree quality: 2
Cracking quality: fair
Selected by Paul Manson.

Shepherd (left)
Origin: Keytesville, Missouri
Pollen shed: I with pistillate receptivity
overlap, scab: 2
Nuts per pound: 77, % kernel: 51
Shuck split: 2 days after 'Colby'
Nut quality: 2, tree quality: 2

Witte (right) [*Missouri Witte*]
Origin: Burlington, Iowa, ??
Pollen shed: I, precocity: 4, scab: 3
Nuts per pound: 70, % kernel: 50
Shuck split: similar to 'Colby'
Nut quality: 3, tree quality: 2
Origin questionable due to leaf retention
and nut size. Wrinkled kernel.

Yates 127 (left)
Origin: Chrisney, Indiana, ~1990
'Major' seedling ('Posey' ? pollen)
Pollen shed: I
Nuts per pound: 66, % kernel: 62
Shuck split: similar to 'Major'
Nut quality: 3, tree quality: 2
Thin shell, good cracking qualities.

Yates 68 (right)
Origin: Chrisney, Indiana, ~1990
'Major' seedling ('Posey' ? pollen)
Propagated by Ed Yates
pollen shed: I
nuts per pound: 69, % kernel: 53
Shuck split: similar to 'Major.'

Dumbell Lake - other (left)
Origin: Burlington, Iowa area.
Nuts per pound: 99, % kernel: 47
Shuck split: similar to 'Colby'
Other selections with similar nut
maturity appear to have better properties.

Grn. Isld. Hackberry (right)
Origin: Green Island, IA
Pollen shed: II
Nuts per pound: 155, % kernel: 38
Nut maturity: 5 days before 'Colby'
Author opinion: unworthy of propagation
due to size, mediocre properties, and nut
maturity.

Snag (left)
Origin: Burlington, IA area
Nuts per pound: 154, % kernel: 41
Shuck split: 17 days before 'Colby'
Author opinion: early nut maturity, but
size, and other mediocre properties make
it unworthy of propagation.

Theresa Foster (right)
Origin: Sumner, MO
Nuts per pound: 152, % kernel: 55
Pollen shed: I, scab: 2
Shuck split: 2 days after 'Colby'
Author opinion: late ripening for a
small nut.

Ralph Upton (left)
Origin: Upton Iowa, 1930
Pollen shed: II, scab: 4
Nut maturity: 6 days before 'Colby'
Nuts per pound: 113, % kernel: 54
Thin shelled, but has generally poor
cracking qualities, scabs.

Woman (right)
Also called 'Old Woman'
Origin: Burlington, Iowa area
Nuts per pound: 127, % kernel: 44
Nut maturity: 6 days before 'Colby'
Author opinion: not extensively
propagated.

RELATIVE SHUCK SPLIT DATES

No.	Cultivar	Origin	Shuck split
1	Warren 346	Wheeling, Missouri	-21
2	Martzahn	Burlington, Iowa	-19
3	Green Isld. Beaver	Green Island, Iowa	-18
4	Snaps	Pleasant Creek, Iowa	-17
5	Carlson 3	New Boston, Illinois	-17
6	Snag	Kingston, Iowa	-17
7	Lucas	Lucas, Ohio	-11
8	Starking H. Giant	Brunswick, Missouri	-9
9	Campbell's NC4	Niagra area, Ontario, Canada	-8
10	Deerstand	Burlington area, Iowa	-8
11	Mullahy	Burlington, Iowa	-8
12	Dumbell Lake-large (best)	Burlington, Iowa	-7
13	Bolten's S24	Indiana	-7
14	Ralph Upton	Upton, Iowa	-7
15	Shoals West	Chillicothe, Missouri	-7
16	Gibson	New Boston, Illinois	-6
17	Hadu-2	Hinsdale, Illinois	-6
18	Woman	Near Burlington, Iowa	-6
19	Green Isld. Hkberry.	Green Island, Iowa	-6
20	James	Brunswick, Missouri	-5
21	Canton	Canton, Missouri	-2
22	Devore	Wapello, Iowa	-2
23	Peruque	Peruque, Missouri	-2
24	Colby	Clinton County, Illinois	0
25	Witte	Burlington, Iowa ????	0
26	Fisher	New Memphis, Illinois	0
27	Dumbell Lake-small (other)	Near Burlington Iowa	0
28	Shepherd	Keytesville, Missouri	2
29	Theresa Foster	Sumner, Missouri	2
30	Pawnee	Brownwood, Texas (USDA)	6
31	Goosepond	Keytesville, Missouri	7
32	Yates 68	Hrisney, Indiana	9
33	Major	Henderson, Kentucky	9
34	Yates 127	Chrisney, Indiana	11

Note: Negative dates indicate shucksplit before 'Colby'; positive dates are after 'Colby'.

Chapter 2

FLOWERING AND OTHER TREE SYSTEMS

Flowering

Pecan is *monoecious*, indicating that both male (staminate), and female (pistillate) flowers are borne on the same tree. Pecan is also generally *dichogamous*, which indicates that for a specific cultivar, pistillate flowers are often not receptive when male flowers shed pollen. The degree of dichogamy varies for different cultivars. Pecans are either protandrous (type I pollen), or protogynous (type II pollen). Protandrous cultivars shed their pollen before their pistillate flowers are receptive. Protogynous cultivars shed pollen after their pistillate flowers are receptive. Protandrous catkins are often visible immediately after bud break. Protogynous catkins are typically not visible until later after shoots elongate. Thus, in the orchard, it is important to have both Type I and Type II cultivars present to ensure good pollination. Illustrations of staminate and pistillate flowers are shown on the following pages.

Flower Characteristics — Pistillate flowers produced on different cultivars are often distinctive both in color and in physical characteristics. These unique features can aid in cultivar identification. Illustrations for some of the common cultivars are shown on the following pages. Note the differences in both color and stigma shape.

Nut Development

Proper orchard management benefits from an understanding of the different nut development stages. For example, irrigation in early development stages influences nut sizing. Adequate water in later development influences nut filling. I've seen nuts split open due to insufficient water during the sizing stage, and too much water during the nut filling stage. Pest management can benefit from an understanding of shell hardening processes. Some pest management specialists recommend that shuckworm control be initiated when shell hardening reaches the halfway point. Pecan weevil management benefits from a knowledge of nut development stages. Weevil eggs can be successfully deposited when nuts reach the gel and dough stages. Nuts abort if pierced by weevils during the water stage. Illustrations of different development factors are shown on page 102.

Nutrient Deficiencies

Nutritional requirements for pecan are described earlier on pages 33-45. An imbalance of nutrient applications can cause significant problems in pecan culture. These problems can be caused by either too much or not enough application of particular nutrients. Basic nutritional needs have remained essentially the same over the past decade. A need for the micronutrient **nickel** in nursery and orchard management has come to the forefront in recent years. Nickel deficiency has been identified as a cause for "mouse ear." I have observed that excess zinc may result in the inability of pecan trees to uptake nickel. Illustrations of nutrient deficiencies are shown on the following pages.

Starting Pecan Trees From Seed

Background — Most pecan trees develop from seed. Efforts to start pecan trees from cuttings have generally been unsuccessful. Seed (nuts) from pecan trees experience shuck split in the fall (September-early November). It is not necessary for nuts to experience freezing conditions to initiate shuck split. If the shuck fails to open before the first freeze, the nut is usually not viable as a seed source. Nuts from a tree that grows from the seed will not likely have the same properties as the nut that was planted. Pecans, and other nuts that have shuck sutures may stay on the tree when ripe, and fall to the ground throughout the fall and winter. Viable nuts of this type will be "clean" — thus void of shuck material. If not harvested, nuts will fall to the ground during the fall/winter and go through a stratification process. Germination typically takes place during the following spring. Of course, this assumes that some pesky rodent hasn't invited the nut for a dinner engagement.

Viable seed — Even if the nut falls freely from the tree, it still may not be a viable seed source. Nut trees are often plagued with insect problems. For example, pecan weevils can invade the entire tree, rendering the nuts useless for either seed or human consumption. Infested nuts are typically lighter in weight than viable nuts. Environmental conditions such as drought can cause the nut to be blank, or poorly filled. Poorly filled nuts may fail to germinate, or develop weak seedlings. It's always a good idea to crack a sample of nuts that you've saved for seed to determine the viability of seed that you've collected.

Pre-stratification — Nuts should be cleaned, then dried for about two weeks. A cool dry place, such as a garage or shed works well. If nuts are stratified when still "green," they may rot or mold. Remove any nuts that are cracked. After the nuts have dried sufficiently, place them in a refrigerator, or other cool place until ready to stratify.

Stratification — Soak the seed for about 24 hours. Change the water once. Seeds will absorb oxygen from the water, and will re-hydrate. Place the seed in damp (not wet) sphagnum, or other moist media. Enclose the seed and media in a zipper plastic bag or other sealed container, and refrigerate for at least 60-90 days. Seed and media can also be buried outside in a critter-proof container. Squirrels and other rodents love to dig up planted seed and eat them or cart them off. The seed may also be placed in a plastic container, with moist media on the bottom, a layer of seed, and a layer of moist media, etc. Hence the word "stratification." This process emulates the planting of nuts by squirrels, or natural process of stratification such as soil movement, or snow cover.

Planting — Remove seed from storage. Seed can be planted immediately, or allowed to germinate in the stratification container. Some literature (mine included) indicates that stratified seed can be germinated in water which is aerated with an aquarium pump. Comments from growers indicate that water germination is tricky, and generally unnecessary. I've had the same experience.

When the radicle (root) starts to emerge, the nut should be planted immediately. Long radicles are fragile, and the seed may split if the root gets too long. It's discouraging to find a bunch of radicles that have been dislodged from the seed in the stratification container. Plant the seed when spring arrives — typically April - May. Plant the seed in the ground, or preferably in pots. Cover the top of the seed with soil/media approximately 1-2 times the thickness of the seed. The seed should be oriented as it would naturally lie when it falls. Container grown trees are easier to protect from rodents, and to apply necessary irrigation and fertilizer. Keep the planting media moist until the plant top emerges. Containers should be filled with a commercial potting mix that provides good drainage. A slow release fertilizer with micronutrients can be added to the potting mix. Micronutrients should include: zinc, copper, boron, iron, manganese, and molybdenum. If mouse-ear is detected on the trees, a foliar nickel spray may be required. Mouse-ear may be caused by excess zinc or other heavy metal nutrients in the mix.

Aftercare — Keep the seedlings watered regularly, especially in summer. If planted in the field, keep the area — about 1.5 ft in all directions from the tree — as free from weeds/grass, etc. as possible. A pre-emergence herbicide is helpful, or mulch the area with wood chips, etc. Apply a balanced fertilizer monthly. Apply minimum amounts to avoid burning the foliage. Pecans use significant zinc, and foliar zinc applications will enhance growth. Container grown trees are best planted in the fall after the weather cools. If the trees are kept in pots over winter, protection will be needed to avoid freezing conditions. Roots are typically cold hardy only to about 27 degrees Fahrenheit, and even warmer for seed from some cultivars.

Darryl and Jacqueline Lyons at their farm near Okmulgee, Oklahoma

Options for Establishing an Orchard

Darryl and "Jackie" Lyons are starting a commercial improved variety orchard at their farm near Okmulgee, Oklahoma. Their plan includes grafting numerous native seedlings, starting container grown seedlings from 'Giles' and 'Peruque' seed nuts, and purchasing a limited number of grafted bare root trees. Shown on the platform are hundreds of container seedlings started in 2005. After established in the field, the Lyons will convert the seedlings to improved varieties. The Lyons are the best crappie fishermen (and fisher women) that I've ever seen. I'm sure that the crappie hope that the Lyons will devote more time to their orchard than to enticing their species out of Eufaula Reservoir.

PECAN FLOWERING CHRONOLOGY

Scale (-15 to 15) is in terms of days before(-) or days after initial pollen shed for Stuart

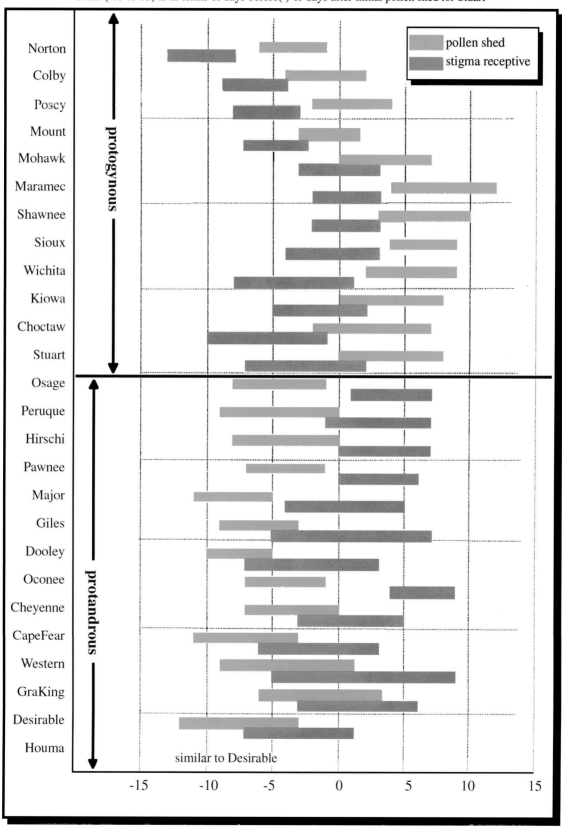

Pecan Flower Photographs

Figure Tr-7 – *Staminate flowers (Type I) of Pawnee during pollen shed. Catkin stalks are shorter in length than those of Maramec (Figure Tr-9). Leaf expansion is also less pronounced on Pawnee shoots than on Maramec.*

Figure Tr-8 – *Staminate flowers of Peruque' (Type I). Pollen shed is nearing completion.*

Figure Tr-9 – *Staminate flowers of Maramec (Type II or protogynous).*

Figure Tr-10 – *Pistillate flowers of Kiowa (upper) and Melrose (lower). Note the purplish colored stigmas on both. Melrose stigmas are receptive.*

PISTILLATE FLOWERS – PROTANDROUS

Caddo

Cape Fear

Cheyenne

Creek

Desirable

Giles

Hirschi

Houma

Major

Navaho

Oconee

Osage

Pawnee

Peruque

Starking Hardy Giant

Western

Pistillate Flowers

Pistillate flowers resemble small nuts, and many have distinctive colors and shapes that can be used to help in cultivar identifications.

Protandrous Flowers

I've found that protandrous (type I) pistillate flowers to be larger and more distinctive than their protogynous counterparts at the time they're receptive.

Protogynous Flowers (6 pictures shown below)

Type II flowers are typically small and often difficult to see.

Chetopa

Gloria Grande

GraKing

Gormely

Jenkins

Kanza

PISTILLATE FLOWERS – PROTOGYNOUS

Maramec

Mohawk

Mount

Mullahy

Nacono

Posey

Salopek

Clark II

Choctaw

Sioux

Stuart

Wichita

Photographs - Pecan Fruit And Nut Development

Pecan fruit develop in several stages, including the water stage, dough stages, final kernel filling, and shuck split. Pecan fruit is the nut plus the shuck.

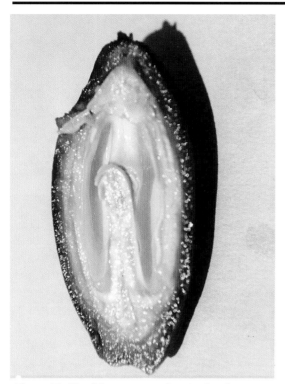

Figure Tr-11 – *Water stage - longitudinal view.*

Figure Tr-12 – *Water stage - transverse view.*

Figure Tr-13 – *Dough stage.*

Figure Tr-14 – *Shucksplit on Major.*

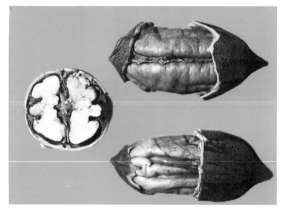

Figure Tr-15 – *Nut views of Western. Top right shows 90 degrees from suture view; bottom right shows suture view; left shows transverse section.*

Figure Tr-16 – *Central partition (left); dorsal view of kernel (top right); ventral view (bottom right).*

Nutrient Deficiency Photographs

Figure N-3 – *Zinc deficiency.*

Figure N-4 – *Wavy leaf margins due to zinc deficiency.*

Figure N-5 – *Leaf scorch due to nutritional imbalance.*

Figure N-6 – *Pecan leaflets before and after application of zinc foliar spray. Leaf on the left grew after zinc foliar spray was applied and shows no symptoms of zinc deficiency. Leaf on the right shows serious zinc deficiency and was in place before zinc was applied.*

Figure N-7 – *Healthy pecan leaf. Nutritional problems for nitrogen, potassium, and other elements are similar in appearance. If leaf color (i.e. pale green or yellow) and leaf structure differ from the picture, a leaf analysis is the best way to define the reasons for the problem.*

Chapter 3

A Summary of Grafting and Other Vegetative Propagation Methods

Additional information on propagating pecan is included in Volume I, page 25-27. A couple of other propagation techniques have surfaced during the past decade, but in my opinion they have nothing better to offer than the three (or four) flap graft for small caliper trees, and the oblique bark graft for larger trees up to four inches in diameter at the place where the graft is to be inserted. Whip (splice and tongue) grafting has a place in nursery environments, and can be done earlier in the season before the bark "slips." Patch budding is also popular, but it requires the bud to be forced after the patch heals. Cleft grafting and chip budding have been used by others, and by myself. I still use the flap graft and oblique graft almost exclusively for pecan propagation done in the field. A summary of the key features involved in propagating pecan and respective illustrations are summarized on the following pages.

Why Graft?

Vegetative propagation (grafting or budding) converts a seedling tree to a compatible cultivar with known properties.

Propagation methods

- **Bark graft** — Perhaps the most versatile graft for fruit and nut trees after the year's growth starts (bark slips). Appropriate for rootstocks 1-4 inches. Appropriate for most fruit and nut trees — except for perhaps some pit fruits.

- **Three flap graft** — Appropriate for smaller rootstocks— 3/8- 3/4 inches in diameter. Done when bark slips; appropriate for pecan and other *Carya,* and walnut varieties — Eastern black, Persian (English), heart nut, and butternut.

- **Cleft graft** — Appropriate for persimmon, apple, pear, pecan, walnut. Best applied just before bud break, but can be applied later. Can be used for small pecan trees where the stock to be grafted is approximately the same size as the scion.

- **Whip grafts** – Best applied to whips – small seedling trees. Best done just before bud break and before bark starts to slip. Can be used for pecan where the stock is approximately the same size as the scion.

- **Patch bud** – often used in a nursery situation, but can be used in the field also. Can be applied when the bark slips in the spring, or in the late summer while the bark is still slipping. In the late summer, buds from the scion can be collected from current growth at the time the patch is applied.

- **Two-flap thick bud graft** – can be used on small to medium stocks, and is described fully in *Pecan South Magazine* – April, 1997.

Early Care – Be sure to label the tree according to the cultivar propagated. Otherwise, you'll end up with "mystery trees." After the graft takes, it is important to pinch back competing growth. You should stake the new graft to minimize the chance of the wind dislodging the graft and new growth. Perhaps, nothing is more frustrating to have a nice new graft started, then lose it to the wind or other hazards.

Later Care – You can remove the foil and wrapping materials in the fall, or the following year. If ants or other insects within wrapping materials start to invade the tree, you should remove the materials and dispose of the bugs. If bug invasion occurs during the first two months after growth starts, re-wrap the graft area.

The Following Years – Train the tree to achieve a central leader form. Gradually remove all growth below the graft by pruning limbs back by about half their length each year, then removing them entirely the third year. Additional removal of water sprouts may be required as the grafted tree develops.

Literature cited

Detailed explanations of the bark and three-flap graft can be found in: Propagating Pecan and Black Walnut in Missouri, Publication 2-2001, University of Missouri Center for Agroforestry, by William Reid, Ph.D. Dr. Reid, Kansas State University, holds adjunct faculty status with the University of Missouri Center for Agroforestry.

GRAFTING ILLUSTRATIONS

Three-flap graft (above)

Make three cuts about 2-2.5 inches long equally spaced around the scion's circumference. Be sure to cut into the inner wood to ensure that the cambium layer is exposed. Insert the scion into the flaps of the root stock as shown on the right. Wrap grafting tape around the entire length of the graft. Apply foil and a plastic bag over the completed graft.

Oblique Bark Graft

The scion is cut about half way through to the pith for a length of about 2-2.5 inches. The cut surface should be as flat as possible. On the other side of the scion, make a beveled cut as shown above. Last, make a chisel cut on the end. Insert the scion as shown on the right. Place the thicker side of the scion against the stock cut. Apply staples/brads, foil and plastic bag as shown on the following page.

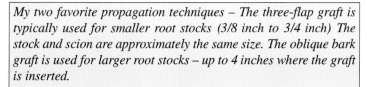

My two favorite propagation techniques – The three-flap graft is typically used for smaller root stocks (3/8 inch to 3/4 inch) The stock and scion are approximately the same size. The oblique bark graft is used for larger root stocks – up to 4 inches where the graft is inserted.

ADDITIONAL GRAFTING ILLUSTRATIONS

Above
Stage of growth about five weeks from the time a bark graft was applied.

Bark graft success! If a graft is successful, bud break typically begins in three to four weeks. Wrappings (first foil - then a plastic bag) can usually be removed in the fall – but can also be done the following spring. Pruning compound (note the black scion above) , orange shellac, or glue can be used to seal the scion. Some people like to use two or more grafts on the same stock to give more than one chance for a successful graft. Choose the most prominent graft and remove the others at the end of the growing season. Be sure to stake the graft to prevent wind damage and other hazards.

A successful three-flap graft! As with the bark graft, foil and a plastic bag cover the entire graft area. Grafting tape or a similar product can be used to tie-off both ends of the bag. Maintenance of the three-flap graft is very similar to that of a bark graft. Picture was taken about five weeks after the graft was made.

Left- Note the position of staples and brad used in securing the scion on a bark graft. A medium duty stapler, such as the JT-21 works best. Use a small brad (1/2" to 5/8") through bark and scion. The upper staple, through the bark and adjacent to the scion, will help to ensure a good fit between scion and the stock. After securing the scion, apply aluminum foil first, then a plastic bag.

Right- It is important to stake new grafts to protect against wind and bird damage. Birds will often perch on the scion, dislodging it, unless the top of the stake is higher than the scion top. PVC, bamboo, or wooden stakes may be used for support. Tie with stretchy plant-tie tape, or a similar material.

Chapter 4

Pests, Diseases, and Other Orchard Casualties

I once heard a comment: "I guess all you need to do to have a pecan business is to plant your trees and wait for the nuts to fall." Ha! Pecan culture is a tough business. There are lots of hazards awaiting the pecan grower. Like people, many other life forms can't wait to ruin or harvest your crop — then cart off the proceeds. Insects, squirrels, raccoons, crows, blue jays, woodpeckers, the lowly mouse, and others can make your crop disappear in a hurry. Beavers, tornadoes, hurricanes, and ice storms can even do away with your trees. Herbicide applicators, if not careful, can also abort an entire crop — or severely damage trees for future years. Diseases such as scab can render a crop worthless. Mother Nature can order up early fall freezes, or late spring freezes that can abort crops, or severely damage trees. But who said farming is easy!

Pesticides

Except in a few areas, pesticides are an essential part of pecan culture. Organic certification for pecan is hard to come by. Pecan orchards where the pecan weevil exists must use some form of insecticide — otherwise, weevils will continue to expand and ruin entire crops. Other pests may be easier to control without the use of chemicals, but crop yield and quality will typically suffer.

A large number of chemicals are labeled for use in pecan culture. I have personally used a few of these to control relevant insects and diseases. These chemicals, often referenced under various brand names, are available from various sources. Please note that pesticide availability, and use restrictions are subject to frequent change. Your County Agricultural Extension Agent is a reliable source for up-to-date information. Note that pesticide labels are legal documents. **Always read and follow directions explicitly. Use of pesticides inconsistent with label directions is a violation of both federal and state law.**

Registered Trademarks

Insecticides are often required to produce a viable pecan crop. Many of the named insecticides labeled for use on pecan carry registered trademarks of the chemical companies which offer the products to consumers. These named pesticides, and the companies that provide them, are enumerated below. The following is a list of pesticides that I have personally used. A comprehensive list of pesticides can be found

in the March, 2004 issue of *Pecan South* magazine (Volume 37, Number 1). Details on how to contact the various information sources is listed in the reference section of this book. For simplicity, I will omit the ® symbol from herbicide product references in the text of this chapter. Listed below is a partial list of current pesticide suppliers and their products.

An excellent up-to-date pesticide reference is
Crop Data Management Systems, Inc.
1-800-237-2367, web site:
http://www.cdms.net/manuf/

Dow Agrosciences LLC:
   Confirm®, SpinTor® 2SC, Entrust® 80 WP,
   Lorsban®-4E, Enable®, Intrepid®

FMC Corporation:
   Mustang Max®

Syngenta Crop Protection, Inc.:
   Warrior®, Abound®, Orbit®

BASF Ag Products:
   Sovran®, Headline®, Pristine®

Cerexagri, Inc.:
   Topsin®

Griffin LLC:
   Supertin/Orbit Agpak®

Bayer Crop Science:
   Sevin® 80S & other products

Certis USA:
   Javelin® WG

Valent Agricultural Products:
   DiPel®

Common Insecticides - 2005

Chemical name	Representative trade names	Signal word	Grazing restriction	Chemical class
1.Microbial	Javelin WG, Dipel ES	caution	no	Bacillus thuringiensis
2. Carbaryl	Sevin 80S	warning	yes	carbanate
3. Chlorpyrifos	Lorsban 4E *	warning	yes	organophosphate
4. Tebufenizide	Confirm 2F	caution	yes	insect growth regulator
5. Spinosad	SpinTor 2SC	caution	no	insect growth regulator
6. Cypermethrin	Mustang Max *	warning	yes	pyrethroid
7.Lambda-cyhalothrin	Warrior *	warning	yes	pyrethroid

* denotes a restricted use pesticide

Common Fungicides - 2005

Representative trade names/group	Chemical class	Signal word	Grazing restriction	Labeled for powdery mildew
Enable 2F (3)	Triazole	caution	yes	yes
Headline (11)	Strobilurin	warning	no	no
Abound (11)	Strobilurin	caution	no	no
Sovran (11)	Strobilurin	caution	no	no
Super tin/ Orbit * Agpak (30, 3)	Organometal/triazole	danger	yes	yes
Topsin M (1)	Benzimidazole	caution	no	yes
Pristine (11, 7)	Strobilurin/ boscalid	caution	no	no
Quilt (11, 3)	Strobilurin/ triazole	caution	yes	yes

The above tables list representative pesticides that are used for major pecan insect pests and and diseases.These are only a subset of available products and enumerate those that are familiar to me. Other products/trade names are available for these and other chemicals labeled for pecan.

Other Concerns
Spray Tank pH

Several pesticides lose effectiveness in alkaline water. For example, the pH of my well water in Osage County, Oklahoma, is about 8.6. To properly buffer the water in my spray tank, I must reduce the pH to 7 or slightly less. I use a liquid zinc purchased from RSA MicroTech, Inc. which will typically provide proper buffering for most of the chemicals that I routinely use when zinc is included in the tank mix. Food grade citric acid is also an effective buffering agent, and four ounces (about 1/4 cup) of granulated product per 100 gallons will reduce the pH by about two units -- i.e. from 8.6 to 6.6. Other buffering agents are commercially available. Several insecticides labeled for pecan are hydrolyzed rather quickly, and thus have reduced effectiveness as time lapses from tank mix to application.

Other Pest Management Philosophies

Integrated Pest Management (IPM), and other user pest management concepts are described fully in the Volume I Highlights, pages 29-33. Natural aids in pest control include proper cultivar selection and prudent orchard management. Trap crops and cover crops are also useful in reducing insect populations. Care should be exercised to preserve beneficial organisms. Since residual effects for the newer pesticides are reduced, proper timing of pesticides is essential.

Secondary Pecan Pests

The following sections describe the primary pecan pests. Additional information and pictures for primary pests, and secondary pests are covered in a useful Guide: _Field Guide to the Insects and Mites Associated With Pecan_, by Bill Ree and Allen Knutson, Publication B-6055. It is currently available from the Texas Agricultural Extension Service, P.O. Box 1209, Bryan, Texas 77806-1209.

Pest & Disease Illustrations.

Pecans and squirrels go together – unfortunately. Several species of squirrels do their share of damage to both crops and trees.

Twig girdler females girdle small twigs, typically in the late summer and fall. Girdled edges are beveled. Twigs contain eggs for the next generation and should be destroyed.

Scab disease prevails in warm, humid climates. Some cultivars are more resistant to scab and associated diseases than others.

Shuckworm pupae protruding from the shuck.

Sometimes, nuts will size, only to stop development for a number of reasons This nut abortion (sometimes referenced as shuck decline) was caused by drift of growth hormone herbicides which caused the gradual death of the peduncle.

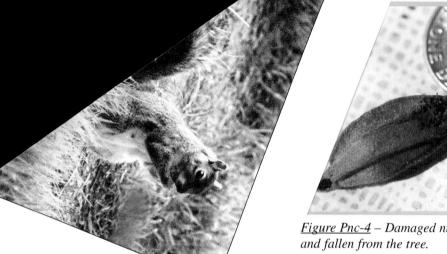

Figure Pnc-4 – Damaged nutlets that have dried and fallen from the tree.

Figure Pnc-5 – Mature larva (left) and pupa (right) of the pecan nut casebearer.

Figure Pnc-6 – Nut damaged by second generation casebearer. Nut size is approximately a half inch long. Note the entry hole at the nut base.

Figure Pnc-2 – Casebearer egg on the tips of immature nuts. The lower photo shows an enlarged view of an egg after it turns a pinkish color.

Figure Pnc-3 – Nut cluster contaminated by a feeding pecan nut casebearer larva.

Figure Pnc-7 – Second generation casebearer moths (size = 3/8 inch long)

Hickory Shuckworm Photographs

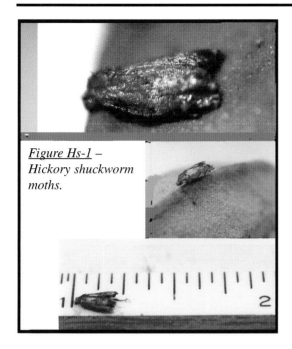

Figure Hs-1 – Hickory shuckworm moths.

Figure Hs-2 – Shuckworm larvae showing resulting shuck and shell damage.

Figure Hs-3 – Pheromone trap used to monitor shuckworm moth populations.

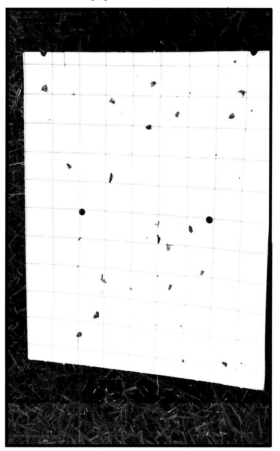

Figure Hs-4 – Base of the pheromone trap showing approximately ten shuckworm moths and a few other insects. Squares are one inch in size.

Pecan Weevil Photographs

**Pecan weevils are often difficult to detect on the pecan trees and pecan nuts.
Photographs of the adult male and female weevil shown in Figure Wv-1 are about twice normal size.**

Figure Wv-1 – Adult pecan weevil, female (top), male (bottom).

Figure Wv-2 – Female weevil depositing an egg. Note the ovipositer on the posterior of the female weevil used to place the eggs into the hole previously drilled by the same female weevil.

Figure Wv-3 – Cone trap used to monitor weevil emergence. (Now replaced by the Circle Trap - see pages 116-118)

Figure Wv-4 – Views of the pecan weevil larvae in infested nuts. Bottom pictures show the weevil evacuating the nut via a self-prepared hole.

Figure Wv-5 – Exit hole of the pecan weevil larvae in a native seedling pecan.

112

Fall Webworm And Walnut Datana Photographs

Figure Ww-1 – *Fall webworm moth.*

Figure Ww-3 – *Mature fall webworm larva at about twice actual size.*

Figure Wd-1 – *Mature walnut datana larva at about 1.5 times actual size.*

Figure Ww-2 – *Fall webworm at different stages of development.*

Figure Wd-2 – *A typical colony of young walnut datana larvae feeding on pecan leaves.*

Photographs Of Beneficial Organisms

Figure Bn-2 – Green lacewing.

Figure Bn-3 – Brown lacewing.

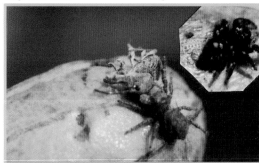

Figure Bn-4 – Spiders of the pecan.

Figure Bn-1 – Wheel bug: top view shows a typical egg cluster; middle view shows nymphal form; and lower view shows the adult.

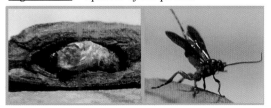

Figure Bn-5 – Parasitized casebearer larva and the respective parasitic wasp.

Pecan Disease Photographs

Figure D-1 – *Pecan nut scab: (1) top picture shows variability in the degree of scab in a nut cluster. Ratings range from 3 through 6. (2) Second picture shows severe scab that rendered the nuts on this tree worthless. Ratings range from 6 through 8. (3) Third picture shows severe scab on Western Schley. Nut shows a secondary infection of powdery mildew in addition to the scab.*

Nuts in all three pictures had no fungicide treatment.

Figure D-2 – *Pecan leaf scab – rating range from "3" to "4".*

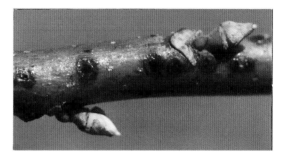

Figure D-3 – *Scab lesions on a dormant Western Schley shoot.*

Figure D-4 – *Scab on immature 'Wichita' nut cluster (July 25, 1993). Leaves were not infected. Note the variability in the degree of scab among the nuts in the cluster.*

Weevil entry. *The weevil uses it's proboscis like a drill, and walks encircling the center hole to pierce the nut – leaving a target-like pattern.*

Figure WC-1 – Circle Weevil trap, *developed by Edmund Circle, Strauss, Kansas. Weevils are attracted by the dark color of the trunk. Their natural inclination is to climb upwards and thus get trapped in the capped cylinder on top of the cone.*

Weevils caught in the top of a Circle weevil trap

Pecan Weevil

Perhaps no other pest is more devastating to the pecan grower than the pecan weevil. If left untreated, weevils can ruin an entire crop. Many people think that pecan insects come from far off places — maybe even Mars or possibly Jupiter. Little do they realize that many generations of weevils live their entire lives in and under the tree that their ancestors staked out. Thus, it is very important to control current populations to avoid regeneration and yearly expansion of the species. If left unchecked, populations will continually increase and spread to other areas of the orchard.

Pecan Weevil Life Cycle

Do we start with the weevil or the egg? Egg laying by adult pecan weevil females begins about 5 days after they emerge from the earth. For egg lay to be successful, the pecans must be in the gel stage or later. To deposit eggs in pecan, a female weevil feeds through the shuck and into the shell and kernel where she excavates a small cavity in the developing kernel. She turns around and with her ovipositor, places three to four eggs per nut in the developing kernel. A female can lay up to about 75 eggs in her life at a rate of about three to four eggs per day. Each female can deposit eggs in up to thirty nuts during her three to four week life. Female weevils cannot lay eggs in nuts after shuck split. Larvae hatch and feed in the kernel during their four larval instars. In layman's terms, an instar is a life cycle between molts. In other words, the larvae gets too big for its skin, and grows a new and bigger one.

The duration of the first three instars is about 13-15 days, while the 4th instar may feed for about five to nine days. Weevil larvae bore a hole in the nut and drop to the ground. Sometimes, the nut will fall to the ground, before weevils emerge — thus it is important to burn or otherwise destroy weevil infested nuts. After emerging from the nut, the larva enters the soil, and lies dormant for one to two years before it pupates. Based on these numbers, the time from egg to last instar is about two weeks. The time from hatch (yielding a mature weevil as shown on page 112) to emergence from the nut is about two to three weeks. After the larvae leave the tree and burrow into the soil, they construct earthen cells in which they remain in diapause until pupation the following season. About 10% will wait two seasons before pupating. Pupae are found in the soil generally from mid September through the first week of October. After transformation from the pupa stage, the adults remained inactive within their earthen cells and do not attempt emergence until late summer of the following year. Thus the period from soil entry to emergence is typically about two years. After emergence, adult male pecan weevils live up to two weeks and up to three weeks or more for females. Female weevils that emerge early in the season can live a week or so longer than later emerging weevils. Thus, females are capable of surviving until nuts become acceptable for oviposition. This basic technical information was graciously provided by *Dr. Phil Mulder, Oklahoma State University.*

Weevil behavior and trapping

Pecan weevils are mysterious, or so they seem to be. When I first saw a pecan weevil, It looked to be as slow as a snail. I was wrong! Weevils can scamper at a pretty fast clip. Their affinity for dark objects such as tree trunks, and their desire to scamper rather than fly, provides a method that allows us to trap the critters before they enter the tree canopy. Besides providing information for an effective spray program, every weevil trapped is one less to puncture our pecans. Having tried cone traps and "Teddars" pyramid traps, I've found that I prefer the "Circle" traps. See the following description. One thing more. I thought I trapped some of the dumbest weevils in the world because they climbed a tree that didn't have a single nut. I found out later that weevils that climb a bare tree simply use that tree as a launching pad to enter another tree. Yes, weevils can fly.

Damage

Pecan weevils emerge beginning in mid to late summer. When feeding on nuts still in the water stage, punctured nuts leak fluids and are aborted. Any eggs deposited in nuts at this stage are not viable, and will not hatch. Some say that female weevils are smart enough not lay eggs in nuts at this stage of development. The main damage done by weevils occurs from the gel stage until shuck split. Nuts infested at this stage are completely ruined by the white, legless larvae that develop within the nut. Larvae later exit the nut and drop to the ground to later pupate, ensuring a good supply of adult weevils to contaminate future crops.

Circle Weevil Trap

Basis for the trap — Weevils and curculios typically exit the ground in late summer and head for the nearest dark object — which is usually the nearest tree trunk. Some say that they come out after a rain or irrigation, but I've found that the toughest of weevils can bore through ground that resembles cement. They scurry up the trunk — proboscis pointing upward, sniffing or otherwise searching for nuts. If there is only one cluster of nuts in the tree, these rascals will find it. They enter the tree canopy and start hunting for nuts to fill their bellies and to lay their eggs. One weevil can contaminate up to thirty nuts. That is —- unless you have a handy-dandy Circle trap to interrupt their journey. Weevils have a tendency to go upwards, and once started, will seldom turn around or go sideways. They get trapped in the top and can't figure a way to enter the same hole they exited. Thank goodness for dumb weevils. Of course there are a few smart weevils that fly into the tree and bypass the trap, but usually only about ten percent of the population have their pilot's license. It is said that weevils are protective of their domain, and no other weevil will lay eggs in the "home nut" of another weevil.

How to build your own Circle Trap

1. Folks, this is kind of complex. If you've had trouble putting your child's bicycle together on Christmas eve, don't even attempt it. I recommend purchasing a trap or two for use as a model. After you build one or two of these things, the purchase price will look like a bargain.

2. If you can work with gloves on your hands, put on a pair of gloves. Working with screen is like wrestling a porcupine.

Circle Weevil Trap Assembly

Stage 1 – Folds and cuts.
Fold the top edge such that it opens on the top side of the screen. Fold the three remaining sides under. The wire (step 14) is inserted under the two side folds.

Stage 2 – Assembly
After attaching the two laths, the trap will resemble the illustration at the right.

Stage 3 – Final Assembly
Your finished trap! Glue the boll weevil trap securely to the screen. In other words, don't skimp on your glue. It's helpful to drill a small hole (i.e. 1/8 inch) through the longer lath before inserting the screw, which anchors the trap to the tree. This minimizes the chance of splitting the lath.

3. I strongly recommend purchasing boll weevil traps for the trap top. These are currently available from GEMPLERS, 800-382-8473. Gempler number R17202. Another source is: Jim Hansel, Great Lakes IPM, 800-235-0285.

4. Dr. Phil Mulder, Oklahoma State University Entomologist, usually can direct you to a source for weevil traps (2005).

5. A jar, plastic or glass, can also be used as a top. Attach a canning jar ring to the screen base using a glue gun. I have trapped more weevils using the boll weevil trap top. I guess the weevils don't want to be preserved like green beans.

6. Purchase heavy duty aluminum screen, 30 inch width. Cut lengths 21 inches deep.

7. Fold over all sides of the screen approximately one inch.

8. Cut two laths, one about 10.5 inches long; the other about 14 inches long.

9. Fold over one side of the screen (30 inch side) at its mid-point, and attach to the shorter lath with a staple gun. Line up the bottom of the screen with the bottom of the lath. The lath will not reach to the apex of the screen cone.

10. Fold over the other side of the screen, and attach to the same lath, forming a cone.

11. Attach the longer lath to the bottom of the opposite side of the screen, again at its midpoint. Both laths should be on the inside of the cone.

12. If using the boll weevil trap top, cut the top out of the cone, leaving about an inch width of screen above the laths. Push the boll weevil top through the inside of the cone, and fasten it with a glue gun. Enlarge the hole in the top of the boll weevil trap to about three-eighths inch diameter — unless you want to spare overweight weevils and only catch the skinny ones.

13. If using a jar as top, attach a canning ring to the screen with a bunch of glue, leaving a small opening (3/8 inch or so) in the cone top for the weevils to exit their screen funnel and enter the jar.

14. Place a piece of stiff wire, centered on the small lath and stapled with a paper stapler inside the fold of the screen front. A little glue also helps this process. I terminate the wire an inch and a half from each end, leaving a space between the end of the wire and the end of the screen.

15. If you figured all this out, you are now ready to attach the trap to the tree. Use a 4 inch screw to attach the longer lath to the tree trunk. I insert the screw only far enough (an inch or so) to anchor the trap. The protruding portion will help keep the trap open on smaller trees.

16.. Staple the bottom of the screen to the tree. I use 9/16 inch staples. I also use a piece of plate foam (purchased from a lumber yard). This is usually blue stuff that's 3.5 inches wide and about 1/4 inches thick. One roll costs about $5, and will handle more traps than you can easily install. Place this blue stuff - cut about 1/2 inches wide-between the base of the screen and the tree trunk

to seal off any spaces between the bark and the screen. Or, if you have a bow knife, and want to skin your knuckles, you can trim off some of the rough bark before attaching the screen — thus omitting the need for foam. Weevils are notorious for going under your trap if there are any spaces for them to do so. You can also caulk any gaps.

17. If all this goes correctly, you trap will resemble the earlier picture in figure WC-1, page 116.

18. Empty your trap every few days Beware of 'possum playing' weevils. It's wise to smush even those that look dead. Weevils also smell about as bad as a skunk — dead or alive. I place a catch container under the trap when I empty it to avoid having to catch the same weevils again.

19. I have caught over two hundred weevils in a single trap in a single season.

20. Other screen widths can also be used to construct Circle weevil traps. Cut the screen length and laths in the same proportion as for the 30 inch screen width.

Weevil Control

Several insecticides are currently on the list for pecan weevil control. Included are:

SEVIN, MUSTANG MAX, WARRIOR. Sevin is a well known formulation of carbaryl. Warrior and Mustang Max are synthetic pyrethroids, and other similar products are labeled for use on pecan. Sevin, the long recommended insecticide for weevil control, is quoted as the most expensive treatment per acre — but also carries the longest residual activity (up to two weeks). Also, pay close attention to alkaline hydrolysis, described earlier in this chapter, which can reduce the effectiveness of your spray programs.

Pecan Nut Casebearer

The pecan nut casebearer (sometimes referenced as **PNC or pnc** is an early season pest that first destroys nuts in their early development stage. Three and sometimes four generations occur during a year. The first generation is usually the most damaging.

The adult pecan nut casebearer is a grayish to brownish moth about three-eighths inches long. It has a tuft of darker scales across its wings about a third of the way down its body. Pictures of the adult moths are shown earlier in *figures Pnc-1 and Pnc-7, page 110*.

Casebearer eggs are elliptical, whitish in color, and are best observed with a hand lens. They are laid singly on the tips of nuts, often on the stigma. As the eggs age, they turn a pinkish color. Eggs are shown in *figure Pnc-2*.

Larvae develop initially as small light colored caterpillars, and change gradually to dark jade green specimens that are half to five-eighths inches long. Larvae are seldom seen since they live most of their lives inside the pecan nutlets. Pupation takes place in a hollowed out nutlet. Larvae and pupae are illustrated in *figure Pnc-5*.

Casebearer presence is most obvious from the invaded nutlets. Damaged nutlets are connected with silken webs. Webs contain small cases and brownish frass. Entry holes in the nutlets are small, and are almost always in the base of the nutlet. Nutlets will dry up after feeding takes place, and are often held on the tree only by the silken web. Damaged nutlets are shown in *figures Pnc-3 and Pnc-4*.

Occurrence

Casebearer larvae overwinter in tiny cocoon-like cells (hibernaculum) at the base of a pecan bud. Larvae emerge early in the spring about the time of bud break, and initially feed on developing buds. A few days after emergence and feeding, they may either tunnel into a new tender terminal shoot or seek shelter in a bark crevice to pupate.

Adult moths from these over-wintering larvae emerge about the time of pollination, usually mid-May to mid-June — depending on the geographical location and weather conditions. The moths mate and lay their eggs singly on the nutlet tips. Larvae that develop from these eggs are designated as "first generation" casebearers.

Upon hatching, these first generation larvae migrate from the nutlet tip down to the nearest bud for a short meal, then back to the base of the nutlet to resume feeding. This journey provides the best opportunity for control via sprays. Each larva eats the insides of successive nuts in one or more clusters until mature. Larvae pupate in one of the hollowed-out nutlets.

Adult casebearers hatch about two weeks after pupation, and the next generation begins. Since the nuts are growing larger with each successive generation, fewer nuts are damaged by the developing larvae as the season progresses.

Damage

Damage is caused by the casebearer larvae. Entire clusters can be destroyed early in the season, while damage is often restricted to a single nut later in the season. It all depends on how big the pecan is, and how much pecan meat is needed to fill up a casebearer larva until it pupates.

Detection

Casebearers may be detected by looking for eggs on the nutlet tips, or by scouting for adult moths. Many pecan producing states predict casebearer emergence by mathematical models based on heat units and other factors. Pheromone based traps aid in pecan nut casebearer detection.

Internet models are available to aid the grower in predicting when casebearers begin their egg laying cycle. Although the model uses Oklahoma Mesonet sites, the general process may be of interest to growers in other locations. Visit http://agweather.mesonet.org for further information.

Monitoring systems, which use a pheromone contained in a shelter, are also helpful in detecting when casebearers enter the orchard. Sources for these systems are listed at the end of this section.

Control

Chemical pesticides are effective in controlling the adult casebearer moth. Larvae are protected from insecticides while they're feeding within the nutlet. They are vulnerable to chemical agents such as LORSBAN-4E any time they're exposed. Biological agents such as JAVELIN-WG, CON-FIRM, and other Insect Growth Regulators (IGR) must be ingested in sufficient quantities when the larvae do their very limited feeding on leaf buds, or entering the nut. With this reduced vulnerability, proper timing is extremely important for adequate casebearer control. Other insecticides labeled at present for pnc control are: INTREPID 2F, DIPEL ES, SPINTOR 2SC, and ENTRUST 80 WP.

Biological insecticides are best sprayed when casebearer eggs turn pink. LORSBAN- 4E or other chemical agents can be applied when eggs, larval activity, or adult moths are observed in the orchard. Some references indicate that sprays may be effectively applied when nutlet tips turn brown.

Hickory Shuckworm

Description

The hickory shuckworm is the larva of a small grayish brown (or brownish gray) moth. Some references indicate that the moth is about three-eighths of an inch long, but I've never seen one that exceeds a quarter-inch. Pictures of the adult hickory shuckworm moth and larvae are shown earlier on page 111. Moths are nocturnal, and are thus difficult to detect during daylight hours.

Eggs are laid singly on the pecan shuck surface, and are sealed with a whitish varnish-like material produced by the female moth. Eggs are tiny, so the whitish colored spot is the best indicator of shuckworm presence.

Hatching larvae begin burrowing immediately into the nut shuck. They develop into cream color worm-like creatures that may reach a half-inch in length. Inconspicuous black spots are present on the larvae's undersides.

Occurrence

Mature larvae over-winter in old pecan shucks or in infested nuts that either stay on the tree, or fall to the orchard floor. Surviving larvae pupate in the early spring, and some later emerge as adult moths. Larvae may also be found in phylloxera galls during the early spring.

Emerging moths mate and deposit eggs on both pecan and hickory nut shucks. Early shuckworm generations have a low survival rate. Before shell hardening, shuckworm larvae burrow through the shuck and into the pecan's interior, causing the nuts to abort and the larvae to die. Three to five generations of shuckworms may occur in a given year.

After shell hardening begins, larvae typically remain within the shuck and feed until mature. Nuts stay on the tree, and most shuckworms complete their life cycle. Mature larvae chew a small exit hole in the shuck and then pupate. (Illustrated on page 109). Pupal skins can often be seen sticking partially out of exit holes. Adults hatch, and the next cycle begins.

Damage

Most significant damage occurs after shell hardening. On a calendar basis, this is typically in August through mid-October. I've even seen tiny immature larvae in frozen shucks late in winter.

Shuckworm damage to the shuck interferes with kernel development, generally reducing nut quality and filling. Damaged shucks also stick to the shell in places. Shells are discolored, and the nuts process poorly.

Detection

Since shuckworm moths are small and nocturnal, they are often difficult to detect. Pheromone traps are probably the best means of visual detection. Careful examination of dropped nutlets early in the year may aid in determining if shuckworms are present in the orchard. Nuts that are aborted by shuckworms will have a faint powdery white stain around the tiny entry hole. Dried spittlebug froth is sometimes confused with shuckworm stain.

After shell hardening, larvae may be detected by scraping away sunken or other abnormal shuck areas. The inside of the shuck will be degenerated and black. The larvae causing the problem may also be there. Shucksplit will be poor and delayed on infested nuts.

Monitoring systems, which use a pheromone contained in a shelter, are also helpful in detecting when shuckworms enter the orchard. Sources for these systems are listed at the end of this section.

Control

Since larvae are well protected from the time they hatch until the time they pupate, control of the hickory shuckworm may be difficult. There are differences of opinion on the value of an insecticide coating on the husk prior to egg laying. My experience indicates that good control can be obtained with the use of CONFIRM or similar Insect Growth Regulators, if applied at the proper time.

LORSBAN 4E, SEVIN, or other labeled insecticides applied when shuckworm moths are present, are also an acceptable method of control. Two or three treatments 10 to 14 days apart are often needed. Burning old shucks and related debris is also an effective control measure.

If shuckworms are prevalent, some references indicate that sprays should be initiated when shell hardening is about half complete, and continued at approximate ten to fourteen day intervals until populations are reduced to an acceptable level. Shells begin formation at the tip of the nut, and harden last at the base (stem) end. Half complete shell hardening can be determined by starting a knife cut through the base of the nut and continuing until resistance is felt. If resistance occurs at the half way point, then shell hardening is half complete.

Stink Bugs & Leaf Footed Bugs

Description

The three primary types of these bugs that damage pecan nuts are familiar by their unique smell when smashed. The leaffooted bug, brown stink bug, and the southern green stink bug are approximately a half inch long, with the leaffooted bug being somewhat longer, but with a narrower body. The leaffooted bug has distinctive long flattened legs. Adults of all types are winged and can fly..

Eggs are laid on grass, leaves or stems of weeds, or in agricultural crops. Laid in clusters of about ten to twenty, the eggs resemble tiny drums. They are yellowish in color and typically have reddish stripes or spots. Stink bug nymphs are wingless, and hang out in small groups. They feed on grass, weeds, and cultivated plants. Nymphs are almost never seen on pecan trees.

Occurrence

Adult stink bugs and leaffooted bugs prey on pecans both before and after shell hardening. They are typically seen on pecan trees in late August and September. Adults over-winter in bark crevices, fence rows, and debris. Nymphs are of no consequence to the pecan grower until they mature into adults and move into pecan trees to feed.

Damage

Stink bugs and leaffooted bugs puncture the shuck and nut shell, and feed on the inner material. Before shell hardening, the nuts bleed and abort. After shell hardening, the nuts stay on the tree but kernels will have dark bitter spots. The damage reduces the value of the nut, and in some cases renders it worthless.

Control

These bugs are easiest to control in the nymphal form before they enter the pecan trees. Removal of weeds and debris and clearing bushy fence rows are also helpful. Check trees that border croplands and hay fields. Apply synthetic pyrethroids or other labeled sprays to the host cover or trap crop, or to the pecan trees as soon as possible after the bugs are seen. As always, spray carefully to minimize damage to beneficials.

FOLIAGE & TWIG/BRANCH FEEDERS

Fall Webworm

Webs and webworms are shown in *figures Ww-2 and Ww-3, page 113.* Here, a picture is worth the hundred words that it takes to describe them. The worms hatch from a mass of eggs deposited on a pecan leaf (usually the under side) by a female moth. The eggs, which are buff colored and protected with a scaly substance, hatch into a colony of tiny worms. The worms begin eating and spinning webs immediately. They grow rapidly and expand their webs to other leaves and limbs. Trees can be severely defoliated if the worms are left unchecked. Mature webworms may reach 1.5 inches in length. Upon maturity, the worms fall or migrate to the ground where they pupate. Second generation pupae over-winter in the soil and emerge usually in early June. A second brood emerges in the August time frame. The adult is a white moth that reaches up to an inch in length, and is illustrated in *figure Ww-1.*

Detection

The webworm larvae are relatively easy to spot on the tree. Sometimes the egg masses can be detected and destroyed before they hatch. Also, the adult moths are distinctive, especially in flight. They look snowy white, and have a wing span of about an inch and a half.

Damage

Webworms can defoliate large and small trees alike. During the late 1980's, many unmanaged pecan and walnut trees in northern Texas and Oklahoma were left without a leaf. Groves resembled the Halloween isle at retail stores.

Second generation webworms can be especially harmful in subjecting trees to winter damage. Trees that refoliate late in the year fail to go dormant before fall freezing weather, and may suffer severe damage or even total die back.

Control

During years with light infestations, webworms may be controlled by removing the worms by hand or burning them. In years that the worms are more numerous, or if they're too high to reach, a spray program may be required.

I've had very good success controlling fall webworm with Microbial products, or Insect Growth Regulators.

These insecticides are selective, and they don't flare aphids — which are often prevalent on pecan trees at the same time that the fall webworm is visiting the yard or orchard. SEVIN is also very effective in controlling webworms, but is usually harder on beneficials — which in turn spares much of the aphid population from being consumed.

Walnut Datana

Walnut datana is the second most damaging member of the gregarious caterpillar family. They are harder to detect, since they expand their operation without spinning webs. Like their cousins described earlier, these webless worms can defoliate even the largest pecan or walnut tree if left unchecked. Pictures of walnut datana are illustrated in figures *Wd-1 and Wd-2, page 113.* Young caterpillars are a reddish purplish brown color, and change as adults to a gray color with light stripes as shown in the pictures. A full grown datana larva may reach almost two inches in length.

Datana move downwards in the tree to molt, usually to the trunk or a major crotch. They form a compact mass, molt, then move their now larger bodies up to where the leaves haven't been eaten, and begin feeding again. This process is repeated several times until the larvae (caterpillars) reach maturity. Like the fall webworm, walnut datana pupate in the soil.

The adult moth is a buff brown with lighter brown wings. The forewings have darker brown wavy lines with white borders. They can be somewhat larger than fall webworm moths, and have a wingspan that reaches two inches. White egg masses laid by the females are typically found on leaf undersurfaces.

Control methods are the same as for the fall webworm. Walnut datana larvae are vulnerable to hand inflicted mass destruction when they move down the tree to molt. My grandsons have captured datana masses to inflict misery onto their female counterparts.

Other Caterpillars

Larvae of other moth varieties occasionally damage foliage on pecan trees. They come in various sizes and colors, but typically aren't as numerous or as destructive as the walnut datana and fall webworm.

Some worthy of note include: pecan catocala, pecan cigar and leaf casebearers, leaf miners, and pecan budmoths. These are described in Reference **PM1**: *Field Guide To The Insects And Mites Associated With Pecan*.

Larvae of the pecan budmoth may cause significant damage to nursery stock and new orchards. These larvae are small and have a greenish-yellow color. They typically feed on tip shoots, and damage the terminal bud.

Budmoths and the other caterpillar-like pests are susceptible to the same biological and chemical insecticides as webworms and walnut datana.

Other Foliage Pests

Pecan leaf phylloxera, sawflies, aphids, and mites may damage foliage. Maintaining a healthy population of beneficial insects such as lacewings and lady beetles is important in keeping these pests in check. Chemical control may be required if infestations become severe. Applications of broad spectrum pesticides may reduce beneficial insects/other predators and flare aphids.

Twig & Branch Feeders

The twig girdler and branch pruner are apparently little pests with big mouths that can chop off a twig or branch with amazing ease. In the late summer and fall, twigs and branches may appear on the ground, or seen hanging in the tree. Severed branches and twigs should be gathered and destroyed since larvae or eggs may reside there. See the picture shown earlier in this chapter.

Other minor insect pests are described in Reference *PM1*.

Beneficial Organisms

"The good guys." Besides harboring pests, pecan trees and the surrounding environment host many beneficial organisms. From spiders to wasps to pathogens, these organisms come in many sizes and shapes. Ladybugs and lacewings are other common beneficials. Their one common attribute is that they destroy or consume enemies of the pecan grower. As mentioned earlier, pesticides that control harmful pests can also do a number on the beneficials as well. It is important to use selective pesticides where possible, and time the use of broad spectrum agents to minimize harm to beneficials

while controlling the target insect. Some of the more common beneficials are illustrated on page 114. See Reference PM1 for further information.

Monitoring Systems

In managing insect populations, proper spray timing is essential. Insect monitoring systems provide a good procedure in determining when insects, such as shuckworms and pecan nut casebearers invade the orchard. Pheromone kits are available which contain both a shelter and "sticky" substance, and a pheromone lure. A pheromone is a chemical substance released by an insect to attract another insect of the same species. Pheromone kits are available for pecan nut casebearers and hickory shuckworms from suppliers including the ones listed below.

TRÉCÉ INCORPORATED
PO BOX 129, ADAIR, OK 74339
PH: TOLL FREE: 866-785-1313
http://www.trece.com

GREAT LAKES IPM, INC.
10220 CHURCH ROAD,
VESTABURG, MI 48891-9746
TEL: (989) 268-5693 / (989) 268-5911
TOLL FREE: 1-800-235-0285
EMAIL: glipm@nethawk.com

Pherocon monitoring system for pecan nut casebearer offered by Trécé Incorporated.

Reference PM1

Field Guide to the Insects and Mites Associated With Pecan, by Bill Ree and Allen Knutson, Publication B-6055. It is currently available from the Texas Agricultural Extension Service, P.O. Box 1209, Bryan, Texas 77806-1209.

PECAN SCAB AND OTHER DISEASES

Pecan scab is the major disease nemesis for people growing pecans in humid climates. Although other fungal diseases exist, treatment of these diseases is similar to treatment of scab. While proper management practices can aid in preventing scab, use of a suitable fungicide applied at the right times is almost always required to control scab where it occurs.

Beware of fungicide resistance.

It is important to alternate applications among the different fungicide classes enumerated later. Otherwise, the different scab races may develop resistance to one or more fungicide classes. If this happens, particular classes of fungicides may be rendered worthless in treatment of scab in the orchard.

Selection of Resistant Cultivars

Selection of cultivars that are resistant to scab is an essential requirement to enable profitable commercial production. See the scab ratings in the chapters on cultivars. The lower the scab rating, the more resistant the cultivar is to scab. Some states, including Oklahoma, have a scab model which aids the grower in planning a fungicide program. Maintaining good air flow in the orchard or grove is also a good preventative step. Keep the orchard mowed, and try to avoid crowding of trees. Thin the orchard when necessary.

Description

Pictures are indeed worth a thousand words. See the photos earlier in this chapter on page 115 for examples of leaf, shoot, and nut scab.

Occurrence

Scab occurs on nuts, leaves, and sometimes on other plant tissues such as stems. Plant tissues are most susceptible when they're actively growing. This is typically early in the year for leaves and shoots when shoots are expanding. Young trees and grafts are susceptible over a longer calendar period. Nuts are most susceptible during the sizing period which begins at pollination and lasts typically into July, and sometimes

later — depending on weather conditions. Resistance of cultivars to scab is an ever-changing situation. Cultivars that were once highly resistant to scab are now highly susceptible. Different cultivars have different levels of resistance to the different scab strains. Most fungicide labels provide information on steps required to minimize scab resistance to the different fungicide classes. It is essential to follow these recommendations explicitly, or sometime in the future nothing may be left to control this devastating disease.

Fungicides and Fungicide Resistance

A list of companies which provide chemicals for control of scab is listed earlier in this chapter. Fungicides can be assigned to different **classes**, depending on their mode of action. Classes include: protectant fungicides (organometal), triazoles (sterol-inhibiting), and strobilurin fungicides. Different races of scab can develop resistance to fungicides quickly. It is highly important to properly manage fungicide applications to minimize development of resistance. Some of the fungicide providers recommend no more than two consecutive applications of fungicides from the same class. SUPER TIN/ORBIT Agpaks comprise two different fungicide classes in a single package. This concept is designed to minimize development of scab resistance. A similar product is the SUPER TIN/ENABLE copak, which offers similar resistance protection. This combined fungicide packaging carries a "danger" signal word, and must be applied using a tractor with an enclosed cab. **Note the table of fungicide products for disease control listed earlier in this chapter.**

Control

Fungicide applications will vary both in number and timing. Consult with your County Agricultural Extension Agent, or State Plant Pathologist for recommendations for the current year.

Scab models. Oklahoma is blessed with the availability of a computer model on the Internet *(agweather.mesonet.org)* to assist in fungicide application timing. Recently, a forecast option has been added to better adjust application timing to forthcoming weather conditions. Even if you don't reside in Oklahoma, you should visit the site. It has useful general information in the management of scab, and describes the model in detail.

In other states it would be helpful to check with your agricultural professionals to see if scab models are available on the Internet.

As mentioned earlier, in areas that are conducive to pecan diseases, choose cultivars that have exhibited good disease resistance. Maintain good air flow by controlling tall orchard floor growth, and prune away low growing branches. As always, accurate records of tree susceptibility, previous fungicides applied and their timing, and other applicable data are helpful unless your memory is much better than mine.

Useful Measurements & Conversion Factors

1 acre of trees = 30 square feet of trunk cross sectional area, measured 4-4.5 ft. from the ground.

1 gallon = .134 cubic ft.

1 cubic ft. = 7.48 gallons

1 gallon = 128 fluid ounces

1 gallon = 8 pints = 16 cups

1 gallon of water weighs 8.33 pounds

1 cup = 16 tablespoons = 8 fluid ounces

1 tablespoon = 3 teaspoons = 1/2 fluid ounce

1 teaspoon = 1/6 fluid ounce.

Temperature: Celsius (C), Fahrenheit (F)

Centigrade and Celsius represent the same temperature scale.

9 C =5(F-32)

HERBICIDE DRIFT

There is little documentation relating to effects that growth hormone herbicides have on nut crops. When nut trees are referenced, literature usually considers the "killing effect" of the herbicide on target plants. When accidentally treated, trees may survive, but their ability to produce a viable nut crop is greatly diminished — often for several years. Unfortunately, many drift violations are not observed at the time they happen. Many victims are often unaware of the symptoms of herbicide drift, and attribute damages to natural causes. This section documents some procedures to follow if drift is observed. Also included are illustrations of growth hormone herbicide effects on nut crops, and the trees that produce them

---

May 18 started as a typical spring day in northern Oklahoma. I was burning some brush that resulted from a devastating ice storm that occurred earlier in the year. Many limbs from my trees, some up to a foot or more in diameter, had succumbed to the weight of Mother Nature's icy wrath. Maybe you can imagine what the orchard floor looked like. Over 50 brush piles were finally dry enough to burn, and there was enough green and moisture in the landscape to minimize chances of my fires getting out of hand.

There was a steady wind out of the east, thank goodness. I was upwind of the smoke. I found out later that the easterly prevailing wind was also a nemesis, carrying large quantities of deadly growth hormone herbicides to my unsuspecting trees from nearby pastures.

Since my orchard is in the flight path of aircraft heading to Tulsa, at first I paid little attention to the sound of aircraft. Trees — at least what was left of them — were fully foliated and obscured the plane making the racket.

Once you've smelled the odor of 2,4-D and similar products, it's hard to mistake them for anything else. Also, spray planes have somewhat unique sound patterns when dispersing their chemicals. I finally figured out that the noise was likely caused by an aerial herbicide applicator. I quickly drove to a nearby road to get a better view of the perpetrator who was covering not only his contract area, but much of the surrounding countryside that was downwind of the target acreage. A nearby neighbor was holding a cookout for his Sunday School Class. We all looked at the aircraft as herbicide was dispensed about 1/4 mile to the east of our properties. Odor of pesticide continued, and needless to say, the picnickers quickly covered their food as quickly as they could.

Having been in the path of drift before, I knew the routine. First, the dates and times of application were documented. We tried to determine any identifying marks or numbers on the aircraft. It was a typical yellow spray plane, but none of us could see any identifying numbers/letters. I've heard that spray planes sometimes magically generate yellow tape to cover identification. I guess it must be to protect the identification from hazardous spray.

Next on the agenda was to contact the governing state agency that investigates herbicide violations. In Oklahoma, the State Department of Agriculture (ODA) has this responsibility for drift onto agricultural property.

Effects of the drift were evident shortly after the application, and visual appearance of damage increased with time. I documented the damage with photographs. The ODA promptly assigned a file number, and contacted spray companies in the area to hopefully identify the applicator. An ODA inspector visited our damaged properties and independently documented effects of the spray.

The aerial applicator contracted by a nearby ranch was identified, and a notice of violation was issued by the ODA. All in all, more than 10,000 acres within a few miles of our properties were treated. Most of the acreage was generally east of our properties, and was treated with thousands of pounds of concentrated (86%) LV6 2,4-D herbicide. Prevailing winds were generally from an easterly direction during a period of application which lasted about 3 weeks.

Although the ODA thought the case was a "slam dunk," the aerial applicator later identified a ground application by another company of similar herbicides on a nearby 80 acre tract. The application was a week earlier and consisted of 2,4-D, triclopyr, and picloram. All three of these herbicides are intended to kill brush and woody plants — trees included. Winds during this particular ground application were about 19 mph, with gusts up to 34 mph according to Mesonet weather records. Our property was downwind of this application, and winds were highly conducive to drift. The aerial applicator, of course, placed the blame there, in spite of about 20 witnesses who observed the spray plane, and smelled the herbicide. Likely, damage occurred from both applications. In 2004, another application of the ester formulation of 2,4-D occurred. Climatic conditions were very conducive to drift. Winds in excess of 40 mph were present during periods of the application, and from directions that caused drift onto my orchard.

Application of herbicides inconsistent with label instructions is a violation of both federal and state law. Commercial applicators in Oklahoma are required to be both bonded and carry liability insurance. Collecting compensation for damages, however, is often difficult for a number of reasons. These difficulties will be enumerated later.

Mode of herbicide action

Growth hormone herbicides disrupt normal plant growth, and typically accumulate in the tips of growing plants. Herbicides typically are applied during May, when weeds and brush (including trees) are actively growing. Unfortunately, this time frame is also during the period of pollination and pistillate flower set for many fruit and nut species. The auxin-like action of 2,4-D and other growth hormone herbicides reduces carbohydrate and other nutrient generation through photosynthesis. Even small amounts of contamination can stop pollination and pistillate flower development. Shoot tips where nuts are produced die back completely, as illustrated in the enclosed photos, leaving tiny nutlets to wither and die. Even with initial successful pollination and nut set, developing nuts are often aborted as the year progresses due to the gradual death of tissues that support nutrient translocation. It's very disheartening to watch viable tissue supporting one's nut crop gradually turn from green to brown, inhibiting further nut development. By the end of the year, my entire pecan and walnut crops were aborted. To make bad matters even worse, foliage, new shoot growth, and even older growth was distorted and later died — reducing the ability of the trees to support future crops. Examples of foliage and limb damage are illustrated later in this section.

Herbicide Data Collection

When facing the enemy, it's good to know the properties of his arsenal. I consulted via telephone with manufacturers and distributors of herbicide reported to be in the various tank mixes.

Active ingredients for herbicides that have encroached my orchard include both amine and ester formulations of 2,4-D, picloram, imazapyr, and triclopyr. Compared with 2,4-D, triclopyr, imazapyr, and picloram are reported to be more soil active and translocate more readily throughout the plant. Traces of these herbicides have been reported a year or more after application.

Results of the Spray Drift

As mentioned earlier, in northern Oklahoma, flowering and pollination occur during May. Literature (Reference 1) also indicates that one millionth of the concentration applied to target crops is sufficient to cause extensive damage in the range of up to hundreds of thousands of dollars if drift onto susceptible crops occurs. Reference 2 shows relative sensitivity of different plants to 2,4-D and other herbicides to various plants. Even trace amounts of the above herbicides are sufficient to abort all contaminated pistillate and staminate pecan flowers, and cause any remaining nuts to abort throughout the year. Leaf functions and canopy density are similarly reduced.

Growth hormone herbicides also damage the terminal shoots which provide buds that develop into flowers for next year's crop. As stated earlier, the presence of growth hormone herbicides, such as 2,4-D, picloram, and triclopyr, also alter the generation and translocation of carbohydrates in a negative fashion. These effects can cause a significant crop loss both in the current year, the following year, and perhaps beyond. Damage to scaffold branches and secondary shoots may even reduce crop load for future years, especially for walnut cultivars that exhibited severe defoliation and shoot die back. If the spray drift is concentrated enough, major branches can die back, and young trees may even be killed to the ground. The above herbicides also make new growth abnormal, causing trees to be difficult to train.

Herbicide damage to new growth causes deformation – resulting in bent, twisted, and elongated "skinny" shoots. This results in scion wood that is essentially useless. If left to grow abnormally, trees may have a weak and easily damaged structure. Compared with uncontaminated trees, damaged trees will have more susceptibility to breakage from wind and ice as they continue to grow. Resulting trees may also be difficult and dangerous to harvest. Besides the loss of pistillate flowers, damage to staminate flowers causes a deficiency in pollen. Surviving nuts that initiate development are often aborted due to the gradual death of the peduncle which provides both nutrient transport and physical support.

Filing a Claim for Damages

Having been the "recipient" of unwanted herbicide on several occasions, I can speak to the difficulties of receiving compensation. Attitudes of the perpetrators and their insurance agents vary widely. In some cases, the applicators and/or their agents own up to their mistakes and offer at least some compensation. Inspectors sometimes offer both a courteous and professional approach. In other cases, the name of the game is to blame the damage on others, or to claim natural causes. Inspectors in this case can take a defiant and intimidating attitude. The attitude sometimes changes when they discover that the claimant is no dummy and has done his homework on herbicide properties.

Defining Crop Loss and Value

If a claim is contested, a typical response to herbicide drift is either for the applicator to deny responsibility, blame others, or attempt to "pay off" the claimant with minimal compensation for damage to gardens, trees, etc. This approach is often successful due to a lack of knowledge on the part of the claimant.

A typical comment by the applicator or his agent might be: "Herbicides have little effect on nut trees. I've been trying to kill them for years in pastures that I spray. They might look a little puny, but they still green-up every year." Owners of the pastures receiving the application might say - and I speak from experience, "The pecan trees in my pasture didn't produce any pecans either." My comment was "Goodness, I wonder why!" If these "cheap" approaches are unsuccessful, the applicator or insurer usually hires an "expert" to examine the damaged property. Sometimes, this is a stalling and intimidating tactic. Now don't get me wrong, some inspectors are totally truthful and honest. Others evidently are compensated based on how much they can get a

legitimate claim reduced.

If substantial damages are incurred, it pays to become knowledgeable in herbicide drift procedures and effects, or hire someone that is. The following processes list some of the steps that I follow in documenting a damage claim.

1. I estimate the expected production of crops that I would have harvested by analyzing relevant historical data from the USDA and the State Dept. of Agriculture, as well as referencing production history from my own orchard. These published statistical data are augmented with personal observations, consultations with knowledgeable specialists such as university personnel, and referencing records from my own and other nearby orchards. Production and income records are important in establishing a meaningful claim.

2. Define a value for the crop based on historical sales, and prices charged by other nearby producers.

3. Estimate future crop losses due to tree die back and other plant injuries. For example, ultimate production for young trees will be delayed - thus reducing and delaying income over the life of the damaged plants.

4. Define a recovery plan that returns nut producing property to the state it was before the damage. This might include tree replacement, moving trees with a tree spade, etc. Also note any expenses incurred in removing damaged trees, corrective pruning, and other corrective measures.

5. Document your time and expenses incurred in damage assessment, including film, picture processing costs, copy costs, mileage to damaged properties, and time spent with the applicator's agents and inspectors. These costs are often eligible for reimbursement.

6. In my case, besides the loss of nut production, nursery products (including scion wood), and other associated farm income, much of my research was negated and future publications such as books were delayed. Dichogamy, scab ratings, bud break and associated data that I painstakingly collected was rendered worthless since herbicide damage affects all these data. Financial losses and delayed income associated with disrupted research and publications were also assessed.

Relevant Statistical Data

1. Statistical production and associated records for pecan and other crops are available from Oklahoma's USDA NASS. These records are available in a similar fashion for other states.

2. Other production records per acre and per tree are sometimes available from state university, USDA-ARS, and county agricultural records. USDA NPACTS records often have production as a function of tree age and/or trunk diameter. Oklahoma State University, and other state agricultural universities use a calibration figure of 30 square feet of trunk area, measured approximately 4 ft. above ground level, to equal one acre of trees. Native pecan trees and trees in some improved orchards are spaced randomly, so a direct acreage figure for these conditions is often unavailable. Often, historical production figures for nut crops are quoted in pounds per acre.

3. Note relevant climatological data. Drift variables are functions of wind speed, sun radiation, humidity, and other weather factors. In Oklahoma, the Mesonet provides critical information on these and other weather related factors. Data are collected in five minute intervals from sites across the entire state. Current data is available on line, as well as some historical data. Archived data is also available. Other weather data is available via NOAA and other weather services.

4. Applicator records – Oklahoma and likely other states require maintenance of pesticide records for commercial applicators. This data includes: legal descriptions of the area treated, pesticides applied, dispensing agents, mode of application (airplane, ground unit, etc.), operator name, climatological variables -- i.e. wind speed and direction, and other information. In Oklahoma, maintenance of these records is required for 2 years. My experience indicates that accuracy of these records is subject to human error (either accidental or on purpose). Some records are barely legible, and are known to sometimes change as a function of time. It's strange that records often indicate wind speeds of 3-5 mph, and always blowing away from susceptible properties even when recorded weather information from scientific instruments indicates otherwise.

Collecting Damages – Good Luck!

It's often necessary to hire a competent attorney!

It's amazing the excuses that the perpetrator (applicator) or his insurer can initiate when a claim is filed. Based on experience, the following events have delayed settlement for well over a year.

1. Denial that their insured party caused the damage.

2. A second inspection of damaged property is often requested a year or more after the pesticide application to hopefully establish drift direction, collect other evidence, and determine longer term effects.

3. Their records and documentation somehow disappeared.

4. Item by item dispute on financial losses.

5. Failure to honor loss of use of orchard components for research and publications.

Ways to Limit Future Herbicide Damage

In Oklahoma, locations that are sensitive to herbicide drift can request that the State Department of Agriculture (ODA) evaluate designation of these locations as "restricted areas." Restricted areas are subject ot additional safeguards and monitoring. To initiate a hearing, interested agricultural land owners may circulate a petition requesting a hearing. The petition must have at least 25 signatures. An open hearing is then organized by the Department of Agriculture. Restricted areas have been designated for several areas in Oklahoma.

I also contacted my Oklahoma State Senator and Representative to make them aware of the problems of herbicide drift in our area. A meeting was held which included myself, Department of Agriculture personnel, and my Oklahoma State Senator and House Representative. Follow-up meetings were held to evaluate possible changes in pesticide laws and rules. The meeting included members from the Oklahoma Aerial Applicatators Association, who voiced support to control negligent applicators.

Conclusions

In Oklahoma and other states, drift from carelessly applied growth hormone herbicide applications is an ongoing and often reoccurring problem. We recognize the importance of weed and brush control in responsible range management. Ranch owners have a right to manage their properties to yield the best return from their investment. Weed and brush control is an important part of this management procedure. Perhaps, selection of herbicides which are less volatile and less subject to drift should be used more frequently. Drift retardants are available commercially, and should be used when susceptible properties are nearby. The law says that pesticide labels should be followed explicitly.

On the other hand, orchards, nurseries, grape vineyards, annual broadleaf crops, and yard plantings are highly susceptible to drift from growth hormone herbicides and are often severely damaged even with small concentrations of these herbicides. This damage can cause significant financial losses and emotional distress to property owners. As above, ventures that require the maintained health of woody plants also deserve the right to seek maximum investment return.

Whether pesticide related violations cause physical injury, seriously damage fruit or nut orchards, or simply wipe out a few tomato plants, affected property owners need to take action. Violations should be noted, reported, and processed. As indicated before, application of pesticides inconsistent with product labels (which are legal documents) is a violation of both state and federal law. While many applicators are careful and take extreme measures to avoid herbicide drift, others appear to exhibit little care in avoiding damages to the property of others.

Through education in pesticide properties, and reporting pesticide violations to proper entities, we can hope that the careless and dishonest applicators will disappear, and the many conscientious and honest members of this important profession will prevail.

Literature cited

1. Illinois Fruit and Vegetable News, Volume 5, Number 1, (Preventing Herbicide Drift to Fruits and Vegetables)

2. Response to Selected Woody Plants in the United States to Herbicides, U.S. Department of Agriculture, ARS, Handbook 493

3. Numerous data found in Internet searches using 2,4-D, picloram, triclopyr, auxin, pecan, walnut, pesticides, and other related key words.

4. Pesticide Labels from TENKoZ LV-6, 2-4,D; GRAZON P+D; and REMEDY. These terms are trademarks of TENKoZ, and DowAgrosciences, respectively.

5. Personal communication with Dr. Tommy Thompson (USDA), Dr. L.J. Grauke (USDA), Dr. Bill Goff (Auburn U.), Dr William Reid (Kansas State U.), Dr. Mike Smith (Okla. State U.), Dr. Dean McCraw(Okla. State U.), Dr. J. D. Carlson (Okla.State U. - Mesonet), Dr. Case Medlin (Okla. State U). The above are recognized experts in the fields of pecan culture, atmospheric modeling, and range management.

Illustrations of Damage from Herbicide Drift

Display of a damaged nut cluster. Notice the different stages of deformation along the peduncle. None of the nuts reached a normal shucksplit.

131

'Pawnee' pistillate flowers killed by growth hormone herbicide drift.

Detail view of pecan leaf with herbicide damage.

View of pecan leaves subjected to herbicide drift. Picture was taken about a month after the drift occurred.

Pecan tree a year after herbicide drift occurred. Note the extensive dieback of one and two year growth.

Shoot dieback from herbicide drift.

Left:
Herbicide damaged catkins. Anthers never opened and catkins remained on the tree until well after leaf drop.

Chapter 5
PECAN HARVEST AND PROCESSING

Harvest techniques and equipment vary considerably, depending on the size and quantity of the grower's trees — and of course budget considerations. Once trees reach a size that defy flailing or manual shaking, a mechanical tree shaker is a must. The most common form of shaker is tractor mounted, and clamps to the tree trunk. Power to the shaker is supplied via the power takeoff on the tractor. Other useful mechanical equipment items include a harvester (picker), cleaner, drying equipment, and cracking and shelling equipment. When processing nuts for sale, be sure to check with the appropriate state health organization for sanitizing and other health related factors.

I remember well my first pecan harvest experience. A tree grafted using 'Peruque' scions had finally produced some nuts. I had observed the five clusters containing a total of 19 nuts since inception. I anxiously awaited shuck split, and my first harvest. As the nuts sized, and September rolled around, I took my usual path to the tree. To my dismay, all nineteen nuts were missing! Closer inspection disclosed a pile of "chewed-up" green shucks and undeveloped shells on the ground. I'm sure that a happy squirrel was around someplace, probably laughing at me.

In the pecan business, one learns quickly that a multitude of "harvesters" in the form of crows, blue jays, squirrels, raccoons, opossums, and other creatures visit the orchard - intent on carrying off as much of the crop as possible. If the grower gets up at 6:00 AM, the squirrels and crows will visit the orchard at 5:00 AM. I was told by a wildlife specialist that 'Mohawk' pecans are too big for a blue jay to carry off. He changed his tune when I showed him blue jays that pecked a hole in my big 'Mohawk' nuts, stuck their bottom beaks into the holes, clamped top beaks over the top of the nuts, and flew away. As the saying goes, where there's a will, there's a way.

Thus to beat the critters to the crop, one must shake the nuts to the ground as soon as possible, and get the nuts into protected space. If harvest can't be done quickly, hopefully, a herd of dogs can be hired to scare all the predators away.— however, I've found that dogs find pecans pretty tasty also.

Manual harvest

Until trees in the grove or orchard reach about fifteen ft. in height, harvest can usually be accomplished by flailing the branches with a 10 ft. section of PVC pipe. I've found that one inch PVC works best. Smaller diameter versions are too "wimpy." Larger diameters are too cumbersome for my back and shoulder muscles. If one is really skilled, longer pipe sections may be appropriate, and even taller trees can be thrashed. It helps to have a well trained wife with good eyes to watch for the location of outlying nuts that would otherwise disappear. That is, of course, unless you can retrain your bird dog to smell out and retrieve nuts without eating them. Five gallon buckets are helpful to temporarily hold the proceeds. A five gallon bucket holds from twenty to twenty five pounds of well filled nuts. When harvesting older 'Mohawk' trees, one must place a brick in the bucket to keep the filled bucket from floating into outer space. 'Mohawk' nuts are sometimes reported to be as light as a feather (just joking, of course).

Once the nuts are in the barn, or garage, and out of the reach of squirrels, mice, etc., they need to be 'cured' to remove excess moisture. Of course, I mean the nuts, not the squirrels and mice. Come to think of it though, a cured and dehydrated squirrel has some appeal. Wonder what pecan fed squirrel jerky tastes like! Don't let the nuts get too dry, however, or the kernels will shatter when nuts are cracked.

Mechanical Harvest

Tree Shakers — After trees reach a size that prohibits manual flailing, a tree shaker is a necessity. Tractor mounted versions, as shown in the illustration, can remove all the nuts from trees up to several feet in diameter. The smallest trunk shaker will accommodate trees up to about two feet in diameter, and requires a tractor with about 45 horsepower. Larger trunk shakers are available to accommodate larger trees and require tractors with more weight and power. Other shaker designs are available. These are usually mounted on the front of the tractor, and can accommodate separate branches. Nuts can be shaken onto tarps, nets, or onto the ground. Nuts, shucks, leaves, and small branches come to the ground. The nuts can be manually separated from the undesirable debris, or collected with a harvester.

Harvesters — Pecan harvesters are ingenious devices that are pulled behind a tractor or similar equipment that pick up the nuts, and auger them into a container. Some harvester models are self powered, and can be pulled with a four-wheeler. Harvesters have a blower system that removes light weight particles such as dried shucks, grass, etc. Longer sticks are often removed with a chain link device that lets the nuts drop through. Longer sticks ride over the top of the chain, and exit from the harvester. Unfortunately, harvesters can't separate dirt clods, rocks, short sticks, and bad nuts such as those that haven't separated from the shuck. Nuts must be separated either manually or with a cleaner. Harvesters can collect the nuts quickly, minimizing losses to predators (two legged or four legged). Nuts can be cleaned in a dry environment, preserving both the operator's temper, and nut quality. It's amazing that rain often accompanies shuck split. A harvester in action is illustrated.

Cleaners — Once one bites the bullet to purchase a harvester, it's best to start saving up for a cleaner. The next best thing is to have a friend who has a cleaner with some spare time available. The cleaner can remove extraneous sticks, "pops" (light weight, poorly filled nuts), and other non-nut entities. An inspection table is also a part of the cleaner, which provides an opportunity to manually reject nuts with weevil holes, "stick-tights," the occasional rock, and other rejects. Cleaner functions are illustrated..

Sanitizing, Drying, and Storage — Health regulations in most states require sanitizing nuts before their sale to the consumer. If selling nuts wholesale to retailers, sanitizing is often the responsibility of the party that sells to the final consumer. Heat, a chlorine bath, and other methods may be used to sanitize pecans. The grower should contact the appropriate health department representatives, since regulations are different from state to state. Nuts typically contain excessive moisture when collected in the field or after being sanitized. Cleaned and sanitized nuts can be dried with a drying mechanism which uses heat and air flow to reduce moisture to an acceptable level. Small operations can use drying racks in a controlled, dry environment to accomplish the same result in a longer elapsed time. Nuts can be stored in mesh bags that provide adequate air flow to maintain proper moisture levels until the nuts reach their final destination. To avoid mold, never store nuts from the field or sanitizer in closed solid plastic containers or bags.

Cracking and shelling — Cracking and shelling equipment varies from a hammer or pliers, to sophisticated mechanical equipment. Manual and mechanical equipment are illustrated. In my opinion, one of the better manual crackers is the Texas Inertia Cracker. It is powered by rubber bands, and can accommodate virtually any size nut. The "cracker box" shown in the illustration makes the cracker easier to use. It fits over one's knees, and keeps the cracking device from slipping around. The nut is placed between two anvils, and the rubber band is used as power to impact the nut simultaneously on both ends. The shell implodes, resulting in perfect kernel halves for many cultivars. Mechanical crackers, such as the 'Myers' cracker illustrated, feeds the nuts from a series of pockets at a rate of one or more per second. The nuts are cracked between two anvils, much like the mechanism above, resulting in quality kernels. The process again yields perfect halves for many cultivars. Savage Equipment has recently developed the 2385 cracking system (illustrated on the following page) which is about eight times faster than earlier designs. Power driven mechanical cracking equipment is more expensive than many people realize.

Shelling equipment is also available from several vendors. Most models will remove over 90% of the shell, and displays the resulting kernels on an inspection table for removal of remaining shell and blemished kernels. Newer models include a packaging mechanism, and scales for accurate weighing. Many customers purchase cracked nuts, and enjoy extracting kernels while watching TV, or participating in other activities.

Equipment Vendors

The author is familiar with the following equipment suppliers:

* Modern Electronics & Equipment 318-872-4764 (includes the Myers Line)

* Savage Equipment: 580-795-3394

* Southern Nut'n Tree (SNT)/ Pecan Producers Inc. (PPI): 800-527-1825

* Thompson Industries: 229-377-3074

Other suppliers are advertised in:

__Pecan South Magazine__

4348 Carter Creek, Suite 101
Bryan, Texas 77802
979-846-3285

Illustrations

Mechanical trunk shaker by Savage Equipment

Harvester, made by Savage Equipment, is used by Joe Reinert, Reinert Pecans, Blackwell, Oklahoma

Dumping pecans and extraneous material collected with a harvester into a truck. Pecans will be processed with a cleaner, or by hand.

Pecan cleaner by Savage Equipment separates nuts from sticks, and other extraneous material.

The Texas Inertia Nut Cracker is my favorite device for cracking nuts by hand. A "cracker box" which fits over the knees increases the utility of the cracker — holding both nuts to be cracked, and the cracked nuts.

Myers nut crackers operated by Dick Hoffman, Stillwater, Oklahoma, have provided mechanical cracking for many years. These devices have interchangeable pockets that can accommodate virtually any size nut.

Savage Equipment in Madill, Oklahoma, has developed the "Silver Line" pecan processing system. This system provides high speed cracking at rates up to 500 nuts per minute, plus shelling and packaging. Picture is from the Hoffman Farm.

Chapter 6

PECANING REVISITED

A decade changes lots of things, and still many things remain unchanged. One of my favorite sayings is: "The more you learn about a subject, the more you find out that you don't know." This philosophy is certainly true in the pecan business. I've learned a lot over the past decade since my first book was published. Yet, I'm amazed that most of what I've conveyed is still applicable. I've found lots of truth in Dr. Glen "Cat" Taylor's statements: "Pecans are mysterious, or so they seem to be. About the time we think we understand pecans, and manipulate them to our advantage — the rules seem to change. Pecans can dent your pride, cause humbling moments, and challenge credibility." One must keep an open mind when considering pecan facts.

But still, pecans can be lots of fun — if you consider hard work and uncertainty as enjoyable. In northern Oklahoma, I've dealt with ice storms that reduced my pecan producing canopies by about half. I've had growth hormone herbicides drift onto my orchard several times. I've witnessed early fall freezes and late spring freezes, with severe winter conditions sandwiched between. And so on! Yet I still enjoy seeing shuck split, watching the multitude of birds that visit my feeders, and even the occasional deer that stands on tiptoes (tiphooves?) to reach that last apple.

Like myself, my first four grandsons are approximately a decade older than when I first described my first pecaning experience. The two older ones, Brandon and Craig, were featured on my first book's cover, and found places in my first pecaning experience. Later, the two next older ones, Josh and Robbie — now eleven years old, asked me, "How come we're not on the book's cover too?" Their moms replied, "Well, you guys weren't born yet." The grandsons replied, "How come?" The youngest, Ethan, now three years old, was sure to notice his picture's absence, so he's on the cover too. My wife, Margaret, thinks Ethan is the cutest thing ever. I have to agree.

Josh, Ethan, and Craig live in Virginia now, so their trips to the orchard are infrequent. Brandon, now eighteen, has recently found that the opposite sex is more interesting than a 'Kanza' nut. Robbie, however, still enjoys visits to the orchard. His only complaint is all the panting that our border collie, Katie, does while riding in the back seat of the pickup. Both my son, Cliff, and at least a subset of my grandsons have shown an interest in pursuing pecans as an avocation. If so, hopefully they'll reap the same tangible and intangible rewards that I've experienced.

As I said earlier, adding a decade of age changes things. My trees are lots bigger than when my first book was written. Come to think of it, I'm a little bigger in places too. I've noticed that the ground is further away than it was ten or so years ago, and my same chain saws have gotten heavier.

Trips to the orchard are still therapeutic. I remember when a tough day at the office was soothed by walking through the trees. It's still amazing how troubles seem to dissolve when I turn into the orchard gate.

As a result of my first book, I've gained lots of new friends. It's amazing how many pecan people exist out there across the world. From next door to Australia and China, I've discovered people with the same interests and the same problems. I've met doctors, lawyers, dentists, and people from about every profession imaginable who enjoy the same avocation. They too, consider pecaning therapeutic and a fun way to spend time away from their jobs. I've met many pecan experts in both university settings and in government, and have learned to respect and appreciate their expertise and cooperation.

As you can see from reading this book, I enjoy experimenting with northern and ultra-northern cultivars. The nuts not only taste good, but I feel hold significance in breeding new and better cultivars for all areas.

As stated before, the orchard is the best living laboratory available. I feel that evaluating the many facets of pecan culture in a single location has lots of merit. Maybe that's why like others, I'm what's called a cultivar collector. I have over a hundred different named pecan cultivars, and the number grows each year. In addition, I have a good selection of native Oklahoma pecans – some trees even older than I am.

So that's what pecaning is all about: friends, family, wildlife, trees, nuts, and even showing a profit occasionally. And it can be rewarding!

Chapter 7
REFERENCES, PRODUCTS, AND SERVICES

Pecan technology is a dynamic process. As a result, new reference literature becomes available each month. Except for the few books available, most information is conveyed by Grower Association Newsletters, journal articles, and the Internet. As such, I feel that it is more important to provide documentation about where to seek current technology than to list references that are only as current as the date my book is published. Two pecan specific magazines, *Pecan South, and The Pecan Grower* (at least in my opinion) are the best sources of current information for the pecan grower. Major suppliers and service companies advertise in these magazines, and many have web sites available to provide additional detail for the grower. In addition, these magazines list calendar dates for grower association meetings. These meetings are excellent sources of information, and provide an opportunity for growers to visit and exchange ideas. See the following page for respective contact information for these and other sources.

Books

1. Rice, G. Wesley. 1994, **Pecans - A Grower's Perspective,** PecanQuest Publications, Ponca City, Oklahoma 74604. (Out of print, but available in some libraries).

2. Brison, Fred R. 1974. **Pecan Culture.** Capital Printing Co., Austin, Texas.

3. Sparks, Darrell. 1992. **Pecan Cultivars The Orchard's Foundation.** Pecan Production Innovations, Watkinsville, Georgia.

4. Thompson, Tommy E. and Fountain Young. 1985. **Pecan Cultivars- Past and Present.** Texas Pecan Growers Association, College Station, Texas.

5. **Pecan Production In The Southeast**. 1989. Alabama Cooperative Extension Service, Auburn University, Alabama

6. Bill Ree & Allen Knutson, **Field Guide to the Insects and Mites Associated With Pecan**, Texas Agricultural Extension Service, P.O. Box 1209, Bryan, Texas 77806.

7. **Other books are available from the *Olde Pecan Bookstore*, P.O. Drawer CC, College Station 77841, Phone 979-846-3285. Currently included are**:
   - Compendium of Pecan Production and Research, by Ray Worley
   - New Mexico State University Pecan Handbook
   - Raising Top Quality Pecans (Williams)

Guides and Proceedings

1. **Insects and Diseases of the Pecan. 1979.** USDA Agricultural Reviews and Manuals. Prepared by Jerry A Payne, Howard L. Malstrom, and Glen E. KenKnight. Available from the Southeastern Fruit and Nut Tree Research Laboratory, P. O. Box 87, Byron, GA 31008.

2. **Proceedings from the Oklahoma Pecan Growers Association Annual Meetings,** Edited by Michael W. Smith, Oklahoma State University, Stillwater, Oklahoma.

3. **Pecan Husbandry: Challenges and Opportunities.** Proceedings from the First National Pecan Workshop held at Union State Park, Georgia, July 23-24, 1990. Copies may be purchased from: National Technical Information Service, 5285 Port Royal Road, Springfield, VA 22161.

4. **Texas Pecan Handbook** - Volumes I and II. Texas Agricultural Extension Service, College Station, Texas 77843. Edited by George Ray McEachern, Larry A. Stein, and other contributors.

5. **Nut Culture in Ontario**. 1992. Ministry of Agriculture and Food, Plant Industry Branch, London, Ontario. Edited by J. O. Gardner.

Fact Sheets

Informative fact sheets are available from the land grant universities situated in pecan producing states.

PECAN PRODUCTS AND SERVICES

Pecan South and *The Pecan Grower* have comprehensive,
up-to-date lists of product and service suppliers for the pecan industry.

INDEX

* denotes a cultivar name